GOLD COLLECTION

First published in 2017 by
## columba press

23 Merrion Square North
Dublin 2, Ireland
www.columba.ie

ISBN: 978-1-78218-334-1

Set in Linux Libertine 12/16
Cover and book design by Alba Esteban | Columba Press
Cover Image by Ronan McGrade
Printed by ScandBook, Sweden

# Gold
# Collection

---

## BRIAN D'ARCY

columba press

*My sincere thanks to all who helped in the production of this little collection.*

*Any profits from the book will be given to those in need, at home and abroad.*

# Contents

...........................

# Introduction

I have been writing each week for the *Sunday World* for over forty years and broadcasting on RTÉ and BBC for even longer. I have discovered, over the years, that the short inspirational snippets that I regarded as 'fillers' meant more to the readers and listeners than the main articles. People still write in for copies of the reflections. Little things still mean a lot.

St Paul in his writings frequently made the point that whilst we enjoy the meat in the meals, it's the snacks that keep us going.

That's how I regard these reflections, quotations, inspirational snippets and pointed stories. There comes a time in life when all we need is a small injection of spiritual encouragement.

In this book you will find some of the most requested reflections from the last ten years. I have thrown in a few new ones just to whet your appetite. I thank all the people who have contributed quotations and reflections over the years. Mostly I have no idea who the source of the inspiration is but please take this as my special thanks to you. Never underestimate the value of a good deed.

I hope you enjoy some of what you find here. It is you who have chosen them because I have chosen what the readers and listeners found most helpful. Enjoy.

# Part 1

# Pause for Thought

# Change

One of the most rewarding times in life is when you finally find the courage to let go of what you cannot change. It happens to me often because I have to learn over and over again that it takes only one person to make me happy and change my life – and that's ME.

I learn a lot when things go wrong, as things are bound to do. You know how it goes yourself. Life gets complicated; it overwhelms us; it seems our cup is filled to the brim. It's hard to handle. That's when I need real friends to remind me that pressure can be positive. After all, 'crushed grapes produce delicious wine'.

Yet deep within us is that irresistible pull to what is negative. If I don't transform that negativity I'll transmit it to others. It's like worry – worry is a virus of the mind. The best cure is to be positive.

Peace comes when I step off the treadmill of anxiety and allow the healing to happen. If I'm the architect of my own unhappiness, then I can become the architect of a more productive life. Change your vision and you'll change your attitude. Change your attitude and you'll change your life.

Vincent Van Gogh, the artist from whom I draw infinite inspiration, was crippled by depression. During his short life, few appreciated his work. He had to steel himself to continue painting. His secret was this conviction: 'If you hear a negative voice within you, saying "you cannot paint", then start painting and the voice will be silenced.'

He quoted St Paul, who also had to overcome his many doubts by telling himself, 'I can do all things in him who makes me strong' (Phil 4:13). I'm slowly learning that when I can't change what is dragging me down I need to change how I manage it. Never ruin someone else's happiness simply because you haven't found your own. And the best advice of all is 'never put the key to your own happiness into someone else's pocket'.

# Love Changes Everything

I remember once holding the hand of a lovely elderly woman who was the mother of six wonderful children. After we prayed one night we talked about her children. I asked her if she loved them all equally.

'I love them all, but not equally,' she whispered. 'The one who was weak I loved the most until she felt strong; I loved the one most who was hurt until he was healed; and the one who felt a failure, I loved him until he felt good about himself.'

In these sacred moments I know that love – real, practical love – is all that matters in life, and in death love changes everything.

# Overcoming Fear

In the English language, we use the word 'time' in vastly different ways. For example 'The time is coming up to 9:30', is different from 'I'm going through a difficult time in my life.'

A well-known Irish songwriter, Tommy Sands, put it beautifully in an email to me. He was reflecting on how past experiences often lead to a fear of the future. 'They say that time heals, but time is never there when you need it – the neighbours are.' Friends, neighbours and fellow travellers carry us through life's difficulties. Fear rules our lives only if we let it.

When I'm frightened by the future – and it happens often – I immediately force myself to do something that scares me. That's how I conquer fear of living. Fear of dying is different though. That's a work in progress.

President Nelson Mandela had a helpful attitude to fear. 'I learned that courage is not the absence of fear but the triumph over it,' he wrote. Courage knows what not to fear. FEAR should be an acronym for Face Everything And Recover.

When I'm with people who have lived a long life I listen intently; not only to what they say in words but to their sighs. I watch their smiles and their eyes. That's when I notice fear and love and their incredible faith in a merciful God.

# Guilt

A spiritual writer I admire, Anthony De Mello, says that when you become guilt-ridden, it's not your sins you hate, but yourself.

I don't normally suffer from guilt – Catholic or otherwise. Yet in recent weeks I've found myself fighting those negative feelings. And, as you know, 'a guilty conscience needs no other accuser'.

So it was time for a little chat with myself.

One of my biggest failures is allowing guilt to creep in and take over when things go wrong. That's fatal.

On the contrary, my mistakes should open up the gateway to happier living. Once a person is determined to help themselves, nothing can stop them.

What's in the past cannot be undone. It is essential not to let feelings of guilt linger. To keep on replaying negative tapes won't change what's happened. It was time to acknowledge what I was doing wrong and learn from it. No amount of guilt can change the past and no amount of worry can change the future.

Just turn the page and begin a new chapter.

The best way to avoid making the same mistakes over and over again is to analyse what went wrong in the first place. Once you recognise the patterns of behaviour that led you down the wrong path you're less likely to go there again.

I began by accepting it was all my own fault.

I had allowed myself to become a crisis-oriented person; I left everything to the last minute. I was living on the edge and loving it. Yet I was putting reckless pressure on myself. And that's not me. I like to be prepared. I believe that failure is not fatal but failure to prepare invariably is. Some people work better under pressure – that's how they get their kicks.

I'm not like that.

My motto is to prepare for the worst, hope for the best and accept what God sends. 'We make our plans; the Lord determines our steps' (Prov 16:9). So live for today and prepare for tomorrow!

# Making Peace

Reading about the events of the first Easter, I am struck by how Jesus greets those he meets with the salutation 'Peace be with you.' That greeting is repeated over and over again. It tells me making peace is hard work. It comes about after a multitude of small difficult steps of forgiveness.

Making peace starts today and it starts with you and me. The hard work of peace transforms and renews us through the daily grind of respecting difference. We can't allow cynicism to destroy our spirit.

Be Big. Don't Be-Little.

# What's Right With You?

Did anyone ever ask you 'What's right with you?' I'll bet thousands have asked you 'What's wrong with you?' Those two questions evoke totally different reactions. One motivates you and the other doesn't. One gives you energy, the other deflates you.

I see it when I'm with young adults and, even more so, with struggling sports people. You can cause a mental block in a boxer's head by saying. 'Your jab is way too slow.' But if a trainer says. 'Let's see how we can get that great jab – you have to travel twice as fast,' he'll have a point-scoring machine in a week.

Catch people doing something right and praise them and you'll convince them that there are no wrong turns on the road of life, just unexpected paths to explore.

Philosophers say we don't get to choose how we're going to die. You can only decide how you're going to live now.

I love this legend from Australia. A group of aboriginals had the reputation of being able to make rain with their mystical dancing. When a neighbouring community was suffering from a never-ending drought, they pleaded with the group to help. The rainmakers willingly obliged.

When their dancing was over, the rains came. The leader went to the dancers to thank them and he asked, 'Why is it that every time you dance it rains?' The chief replied, 'It's very simple. We dance until it rains.'

The principle is clear. Shine a light on what is good and keep on doing it.

It's as old as the Bible. St Paul advised, 'Don't grow weary of doing good ... you'll reap the harvest when the time is right' (Gal 6:9).

<hr />

# The Word of God in Your Pocket

From the beginning, Pope Francis said, charismatics were known for their love of and familiarity with the scriptures; the Pope asked those who lost the habit of carrying their bible with them everywhere to 'return to this first love, always have the word of God in your pocket or purse'.

Pope Francis also said Catholic charismatics have a special role to play in healing divisions among Christians by exercising 'spiritual ecumenism', or praying with members of other Christian churches and communities who share a belief in Jesus as lord and saviour.

# Life, Animated

Who would ever imagine that a fixation with animated cartoons would provide the key to unlock a young boy's autism? Owen Suskind's father, Pulitzer Prize-winner Ron Suskind, explains that his son Owen 'has a deep connection to movies, especially cartoons. He's watched them countless times, and through them makes sense of his often bewildering world.'

Owen seemed a perfectly ordinary, bright baby until, mysteriously, at the age of three he succumbed, almost overnight, to a severe developmental disorder. He retreated into an unreachable world of silence and gibberish. His parents, Ron and Cornelia, and his brother Walter, were distraught. When Owen was bullied at his special school, they knew their lives would never be the same again. Yet their perseverance, dedication and never-ending hope helped them rescue their precious son.

It was during a family viewing of *The Little Mermaid* that their Eureka moment came. Owen insisted on replaying one particular scene repeatedly. That's when they discovered that he had memorised the dialogue word for word. Later they learned he had memorised the entire scripts of almost fifty films and cartoons.

On a whim, his dad used the glove puppet of Iago from *Aladdin* to speak to Owen. Using Iago's cartoon voice Ron asked Owen how he felt. Owen spoke back to Iago and admitted he was very lonely. That was the breakthrough.

With their exaggerated emotions, the cartoons provided the building blocks for Owen to make sense of his thoughts. He used the cartoon characters to communicate what he felt deep inside his hidden world.

With wonderful therapy, and heroic patience from his family, Owen has now become a talkative, high-functioning young adult who has found employment, a girlfriend and independent living. He has even travelled with his parents to France to speak about his experiences.

In God's creation, everyone is special and unique. Ron summed up his son's uniqueness like this. 'When we shared Owen's story we thought he was one in a million. Which he is. Now we know he's also one among millions.'

---

# The Temptation to Control

The temptation to become 'controllers' of the grace of God is a danger, Pope Francis says. Group leaders, sometimes without even meaning to, become 'administrators of grace', deciding who should exercise which gifts of the Holy Spirit.

'Don't do this any more,' Pope Francis says. 'Be dispensers of God's grace, not controllers. Don't be the Holy Spirit's customs agents.'

# Loving

I was hoping Ruth Negga would win the Best Actress Oscar in 2017 for her performance in *Loving*, not just because she's Irish, but because of the power of the true-life story behind the film.

Richard and Mildred Loving went through agonies to have their interracial marriage recognised in the US. They had to leave their home state of Virginia and move to Washington to be married in 1958. Interracial marriage was forbidden in Virginia; five weeks after the couple returned home, police broke into their bedroom and arrested them in the middle of the night. Their crime was loving each other enough to celebrate an interracial marriage.

The judge found them guilty and ordered them to leave Virginia or go to jail. For ten years they lived in Washington and cared for their three children.

Encouraged by the civil rights movement, Mildred wrote to Attorney General Robert Kennedy. He helped them find two young lawyers who took their case all the way to the Supreme Court in 1967. The judges ruled unanimously that state laws prohibiting mixed marriage were unconstitutional and the country's last remaining segregation laws were annulled.

The Loving's life story on film could have been full of self-righteous histrionics. Instead it's a quiet, reserved and beautiful study of how love thrives and marriage survives under unbearable pressures. Two ordinary people, madly in love, achieved something extraordinary. In the midst of their turmoil, Mildred wrote hundreds of tender, gossipy letters to her husband. It's an inspiring love story.

*Loving* deliberately concentrates on how an unjust, cruel law affects the day-to-day lives of innocent people – their relationships, where they could make their home, how they raised their children.

Mildred was softly spoken, shy and demure, yet incredibly strong-willed. She was never afraid to speak the truth. She reminds us that the world is changed by people of principle who make huge contributions in unassuming ways. The Lovings survived because they had an absolute conviction about the value of doing the right thing.

They weren't martyrs or saints, just good, decent people. The kind of people we can all be – if we so decide.

## Mind Your Health

Looking after your health is important. St Vincent de Paul tells us, 'Be very careful of your health. The devil employs a trick to deceive good souls. He incites them to do more than they are able, in order that they may no longer be able to do anything.'

# Religion

They say that religion is for those who fear hell; spirituality is for those who've already been there. To put it another way, when fear governs everything I do, life is miserable; when I choose the right thing simply because it's the right thing to do, my life is filled with peace. Attitude is everything.

I've always seen myself as being of average ability at best. I realised early on that hard work would be necessary. Hard work became a habit for me and remains so to this day. Now I'm convinced that hard work will always beat talent when talent refuses to work hard. I see hard work as a precious gift that helps me achieve what I once thought impossible.

The secret is to be content with small steps.

Many years ago a wise teacher gave me the most valuable mantra of all. He said, 'By the yard it's hard; by the inch it's a cinch'. That simple statement allowed me to see that it is better to take one small step in the right direction than to make a huge leap in the wrong direction. I am content to take small steps on the journey of life without getting caught up in destination addiction. When I get tired I learn to rest, not to quit.

As the poet John Dryden wrote, 'We first make our habits and then our habits make us.' Little things make big things happen.

# Making Excuses

You've heard about the dog who ate the homework, but what about the cat who unplugged the alarm clock? There is no end to the creative minds of people who want to find an excuse for not going to work. Did you know that only 40 per cent of absenteeism at work is due to personal illness, 60 per cent for other reasons, such as family problems, personal needs, stress and, most of all, laziness. Here are a few of the more unusual reasons that people used for missing work:

> I tripped over my dog and was knocked unconscious.
> My bus broke down.
> I was arrested but it was a case of mistaken identity.
> I forgot to come back to work after lunch.
> I couldn't find my shoes.
> My curlers burned my hair.
> I eloped.
> My cat unplugged my alarm clock.
> I had to be there for my husband's trial.
> I forgot what day of the week it was.

Don't forget, though, that missing work under false pretences is a very obvious form of stealing.

# Actions Speak
# Louder Than Words

In 1989 I was studying in Chicago and helping out in a parish. The people of the parish told me about a wonderful pastor who worked there in the 1950s. They never forgot him. Everything in the parish went back to him. The story they told me was that when they had nothing in this newly formed parish the priest gathered a group of people around him to advise him, but they were inspired by him.

They agreed that the area needed something for the youth. They took the decision to bulldoze the car park and to put a fine tarmacadam surface on it. It was perfect for basketball. The priest put up basketball rings and then bought the best ball possible so that all the kids could play on a good surface with good equipment.

The parishioners advised him to buy something cheaper because the kids would steal a good ball. But he responded, 'Good basketballs for good people.'

As the people predicted, the first expensive basketball he bought was stolen within three days. The parishioners refused to replace it but he bought one out of his own pocket. This one lasted three weeks. He bought an even better one and it was a full year before it disappeared. He then bought a fourth one. It was never stolen.

I asked them if the priest was a good preacher. They said they never remembered a single sermon he gave. But

each one of them remembered his mantra, 'Good basketballs for good people.'

Actions speak louder than words.

◇◇◇◇◇◇◇◇◇◇◇◇◇◇◇◇◇◇◇◇◇◇◇◇◇◇◇◇◇◇◇◇◇◇◇◇◇◇◇◇◇◇◇◇◇◇◇◇◇◇◇◇

# Letting Go

To let go does not mean to stop caring:
it means, I can't do it for someone else.
To let go is not to enable,
but to allow learning from natural
    consequences.
To let go is not to fix,
but to be supportive.
To let go is not to be in the middle
arranging all the outcomes,
but to allow others to affect their destinies.
To let go is not to be protective;
it's to permit another to face reality.
To let go is not to criticise and
regulate anybody, but to try to
become what I dream I can be.
To let go is not to regret the past,
but to grow and live for the future.
To let go is to fear less and love more.

# An Encouraging
# Word

An encouraging word works wonders for the morale. Why is it that we are so reluctant to tell people when they do well, but eager to condemn them if they fail?

Bob Danzig is now a famous American motivational speaker. He started life as an office boy at a newspaper and ended up CEO of the group. He credits his success to words of encouragement spoken to him at a crucial time in his life by two caring individuals.

Bob spent his childhood moving around five different foster homes. He desperately needed to be loved. But each time he moved he was rejected. At the age of nine he was given a new social worker to help him through his difficulties. At the end of their first meeting she told him, 'Bobby, I want you to always remember these words: You are worthwhile.' She repeated those same words at the end of every meeting they had. In time Bob Danzig began to believe in her.

When he graduated from high school he got a job in a newspaper, as a runner – the bottom rung of the ladder. He had worked there for six months when his superior called him in to her office. He was sure he would be sacked. Instead she said, 'I've been observing you, young man, and I believe you are full of promise.'

That was all he needed. He worked hard to justify the confidence she had in him. In time he rose to the very top of the newspaper industry and he now donates the money he earns from speaking engagements to foster children who, like himself, had a difficult start in life. He does it because he knows that the right word at the right time changed his life.

As the Book of Proverbs reminds us, 'an encouraging word is like apples of gold in a setting of silver' (25–21).

Louis Pasteur put it well when he said, 'When I see a child I'm inspired by two sentiments: tenderness for what he is and respect for what he may become.'

May someone be kind enough to inspire you with a helpful word today and may you be generous enough to pass it on.

◇◇◇◇◇◇◇◇◇◇◇◇◇◇◇◇◇◇◇◇◇◇◇◇◇◇◇◇◇◇◇◇◇◇◇◇◇◇◇◇◇◇◇◇◇◇◇◇◇◇◇◇◇◇◇◇

# The Bones

It has been said that there are four main bones in every organisation:

The *Wishbones*: Those who wish somebody else would do something about the problem.

The *Jawbones*: Those who do all the talking but very little else.

The *Knucklebones*: Those who knock everything.

The *Backbones*: Those who do the most of the work.

# Humanity

I once read a long interview with Jean Vanier. For the last fifty years he has shared his life, and built friendships with, what he calls 'unequals'. Many of these people had intellectual and developmental disabilities and were forced by society to live in isolation in institutions. Vanier found his emotional intelligence and love in the people he shared his life with. He founded the L'Arche movement, and today there are about 150 L'Arche communities across the world.

After fifty years living in those communities, Vanier has enlightening thoughts to share. He says, 'The whole of humanity is built up through experience. And then we reflect on this experience. For instance, until recently Catholics were not supposed to speak to Protestants – theoretically – when we met we discovered that many Protestants are holy people. Pope Francis said, 'Go to the periphery and meet the people and when you meet them you discover something and you receive some of their wisdom ... we define our identity through winning but we can also find our identity through communion with another person.'

He goes on to say that we learn mercy when we experience community. 'Mercy is not just giving food to the poor, it is meeting the poor and risking; there is always a question, where this will lead me? And this means my barriers are dropped and the poor are leading me to something new ... To grow in humanity means to let the barriers of fear drop.'

Humanity is fragile, but wonderful. We are born in great fragility and we will die in great fragility. The meaning of fragility is to bring us back to reality. The reality is that we are body and spirit. And what is most important? It is to work for peace ... and that means other people can discover that we do not have to be in a struggle between power and love.

Vanier uses a wonderful example about the value of relationship from an addict who had overdosed. 'In Australia,' he says, 'There was a guy a long time ago who was dying from an overdose and his last words were, "You always wanted to change me, but you never wanted to meet me".'

# The Guru's Cat

When the guru sat down to worship each evening the ashram cat would get in the way and distract the worshippers. So the guru ordered that the cat be tied up during evening worship.

Long after the guru died the cat continued to be tied up during evening worship, and when it eventually died, another cat was brought to the ashram so that it could be duly tied up during evening worship.

Centuries later learned treatises were written by the guru's disciples on the essential role of a cat in all properly conducted worship.

# The Journey of Life

For each of us life is like a journey.
Birth is the beginning of this journey,
And death is not the end but the destination.
It is a journey that takes us
From youth to age,
From innocence to awareness,
From ignorance to knowledge,
From foolishness to wisdom,
From weakness to strength
and often back again,
From offence to forgiveness,
From loneliness to friendship,
From pain to compassion,
From fear to faith,
From defeat to victory
and from victory to defeat,
Until, looking backwards or ahead,
We see that victory does not lie
At some high point along the way,
But in having made the journey,
stage by stage.

*Adapted from an old Hebrew prayer*

# Setting Out on the Journey of Life

One way of looking at life is to see it as a journey of forgiveness; forgiving others, forgiving God and forgiving myself. The most difficult one to forgive is myself. I journey through life slowly and painfully, step by step, which means I don't have to be perfect now.

Most of us carry baggage from the families we were brought up in. Seamus Heaney jokingly analysed his parents. His mother's motto in life was, 'Whatever you say, say nothing.' She never put it into practice herself because she talked non stop. His father was different. He could communicate, but not with words. Heaney says 'language was a kind of betrayal' for his father.

Heaney wrote his poem 'The Follower' about his father. He sees himself as a boy following his father, a strong man handling a plough behind a horse. He stumbles along beside his father, getting in his way. He wants to grow up, to plough and to close one eye and stiffen his arm like his father. But in fact, when he is a grown man it is his father 'who keeps stumbling behind me and will not go away'. How true that is.

Parents at first are heroes whom we follow with baby steps. But the older we get the more like them we become. Even when they are dead they haunt us. When we look over our shoulder or into a mirror, we find them stumbling behind us as we become more like them.

Life is a journey of forgiveness. But it is also a journey of self-awareness. That's the journey of life and the cycle of life too. When we fail to reflect or make the journey inwards, we get stuck in a rut. I need to know I'm loved for who I am and not for what I do. That's the way God loves me.

There is no need for fear; no need for change. God loves this struggling mixture of success and failure. God loves you for it is impossible for God not to love. 'The end of all exploring will be to arrive where we started and know the place for the first time,' was how T. S. Eliot put it.

# Seeing Things

There is an old Jewish legend in which a rich but miserable man goes to see his rabbi. The wise old rabbi leads him to a window. 'Look out there,' he says, 'and tell me what you see.'

'I see people,' answers the rich but miserable man. Then the rabbi leads him to a mirror.

'What do you see now? he asks. 'I see myself,' says the rich but miserable man.

Then the rabbi says: 'Behold! In the window there is glass and in the mirror there is glass. But the glass of the mirror is covered with a little silver, and no sooner is a little silver added than you cease to see others and see only yourself.'

# The Risk of Love

To weep is to risk appearing sentimental.
To reach out to another is to risk
    involvement.
To expose your feelings is to risk exposing
    your true self.
To lay your ideas, your dreams before the
    crowd is to risk their laughter.
To love is to risk not being loved in return.
To live is to risk dying,
To hope is to risk despair,
To try is to risk failure,
But risks must be taken
Because the greatest hazard in life is to risk
    nothing.
The person who risks nothing
Has nothing, does nothing, is nothing.
He may avoid suffering and worry
But he simply cannot learn, feel, change,
    grow, love, live.
Chained by his certitudes
He is a slave,
He has forfeited freedom.
Only the person who risks
Is thoroughly free.

# A Few Commandments For a Long, Peaceful Life

1. Thou shalt not worry, for worry is the most unproductive of all human activities.
2. Thou shalt not be fearful, for most of the things we fear never come to pass.
3. Thou shalt not cross bridges before you get to them, for no one yet has succeeded in accomplishing this.
4. Thou shalt face each problem as it comes. You can handle only one problem at a time.
5. Thou shalt not borrow other people's problems. They can take better care of them than you can.
6. Thou shalt not try to relive yesterday; it is gone. Concentrate on what is happening in your life today.
7. Thou shalt count thy blessings, never overlooking the small ones. A lot of small blessings add up to a big one.
8. Thou shalt be a good listener. Only when you listen do you hear ideas different from your own. It's very hard to learn something new when you're talking.
9. Thou shalt not become bogged down by frustration. Ninety per cent of it is rooted in self-pity and will only interfere with positive action.

# The Duty to be Happy!

Robert Louis Stevenson suffered poor health from childhood right up until he died at the age of forty-four. But he never allowed illness to conquer his spirit. He felt that being happy was a duty and he faithfully followed a number of precepts to keep himself as happy as possible. Here they are:

Make up your mind to be happy. Learn to find pleasure in simple things.

Make the best of your circumstances. No one has everything, and everyone has some sorrow mixed in with the gladness of life. The trick is to make the laughter outweigh the tears.

Don't take yourself too seriously. Don't think that somehow you should be protected from the misfortunes that befall other people.

Don't let criticism worry you. You can't please everybody.

Don't let others set your standards. Be yourself.

Do the things you enjoy doing, but don't get into debt in the process.

Don't borrow trouble. Imaginary things are harder to bear than the actual ones.

Do not cherish enmities. Don't hold grudges. Hatred poisons the soul.

Have many interests. If you can't travel, read about many places.

Don't spend your life brooding over sorrows or mistakes. Don't be one who never gets over things.

Do what you can for those less fortunate than yourself.

Keep busy at something. A very busy person never has time to be unhappy.

# Coronary and Ulcer Rules

The Coronary and Ulcer Club lists the following rules for members:

1. Your job comes first. Forget everything else.

2. Saturdays, Sundays and bank holidays are fine times to be working at the office. There'll be nobody else there to bother you.

3. Always have your briefcase with you when not at your desk. This provides an opportunity to review completely all the troubles and worries of the day.

4. Accept all invitations to meetings, lunches, committees etc.

5. All forms of recreation are a waste of time.

6. Never delegate responsibility to others; carry the entire load yourself.

7. If your work calls for travelling, work all day and travel at night to keep that appointment you made for eight in the morning.

8. No matter how many jobs you are already doing, remember you always can take on more.

# A Father's Day Story

I once did an interview with Val Doonican. We were reminiscing about his childhood in Waterford. He was the youngest of eight children. The family lived in a small house. His sister Mary got TB. The house was crowded but she needed a special place to herself, and to make room, his father moved out of the house, put his bed in a tool shed at the bottom of the garden and lived there for the rest of his life.

His father was somewhat fond of drink but young Val hero-worshipped him as a man who read books all the time, although he kept very much to himself. Val told a story of how his father eventually had to give up work when he got sick, and still lived on his own in the shed at the bottom of the garden. After school Val, who was then twelve or thirteen, used to sit and talk to him.

He knew his father was sick but his father never told him what was wrong. One spring evening his father asked him to go out and look in the hedges to see if the black-berry bushes were in blossom and asked him to bring him back the blooms.

Val did as his father asked. Later, while putting rubbish in the bin, he discovered, at the bottom of the bin, all the blossoms from the blackberry bushes, soaking wet and thrown in the bottom of the bin. He was horribly disappointed that his father hadn't been more appreciative of his efforts.

Eventually his father went into hospital. One evening Val went up to see him and his face was all bandaged. His father told him that he had a very painful illness in his mouth and that he was not a pretty sight, so it would be better if the young man never came back to see him again.

He said goodbye to him and then called him back. He had one more thing to say to him. He said: 'You think I'm a hero, don't you? Well I'm not a hero at all. I've wasted my life. And the reason I'm telling you this is that when I die there will be people who will tell you that your father was a no-good waster. And I want you to be able to say, I know that, because he told me himself.'

Almost twenty years later, when Val was a singer, he was staying in a B & B in Scotland. He picked up a book to browse through. It was about ancient cures. And when he came to blackberries he read that, in some parts of Ireland, boiled blackberry blossoms were thought to be a cure for mouth cancer.

And it all clicked into place then. His father obviously knew he had cancer and tried to cure himself with the blossoms and that's why he had boiled them and later put them in the bin.

It nearly broke Val's heart. His father was long dead but he suddenly realised the kind of man he was. A silent sufferer. But a man who knew a lot about himself and a lot about what fathers should be.

# The Dragon Within

A man went to a psychiatrist. He had a sad tale to tell. He told the psychiatrist how everything in his life had gone wrong. How he had lost his job. How, on many occasions, he had felt like committing suicide.

Now he was in even worse trouble. He was drinking far too much. There were days, he said, when he felt like there was a dragon consuming him with a breath of fire.

He wondered if the psychiatrist could do anything to help him.

The psychiatrist said he could help him, but there would be two conditions. Firstly, it would take him two years to do it, and, secondly, it would cost him €10,000.

The man was shocked at the suggestion that it was going to cost him so much money, so he said to the psychiatrist, 'I'm afraid it's time I made friends with this dragon.'

There are times when we have to make friends with the dragons within us.

# Stress Points

According to the latest research, stress is a major killer in today's world. Stress comes about when we face more challenges than we can cope with. Not all stress is bad for us and not all stressful events have the same effect on people.

In a recent edition of the BUPA magazine, an article on stress showed that no two people react to events in the same way. Pinpointing the causes of stress is not an accurate science. Sometimes leisure activities can cause more stress than work.

The obvious illnesses caused by stress are heart disease and cancer. But it also takes its toll on the digestive system, lungs, skin, hair, brain, immune system and relationships with others. Ulcers, eczema, asthma, baldness, muscle spasms and nervous breakdowns all have stress as their primary cause.

Psychologists have now compiled a list of some of life's stressful events and given each a score:

| | |
|---|---|
| Death and bereavement | 50 points |
| Separation and divorce | 35 points |
| Moving house | 31 points |
| Marriage | 25 points |
| Redundancy/retirement | 23 points |
| Pregnancy/caring for the elderly | 20 points |
| Changes at work | 18 points |
| Family squabble | 17 points |
| Promotion | 16 points |
| Changing lifestyle | 13 points |

| | |
|---|---|
| Changed working conditions | 10 points |
| New hobby/social life | 9 points |
| Change in sleep pattern | 8 points |
| Change in career | 7 points |
| Holidays and Christmas | 6 points |
| A brush with the law | 5 points |

Here's how you can add up your own stress score. If your total in any twelve-month period exceeds 75 points, you have a 50 per cent chance of a serious stress-related illness. With a total of 150 points, you have an 80 per cent chance.

## Stress-busters

Here are a few stress-busting techniques, all of which can reduce stress and help you gain a new outlook on life.

- Regular exercise
- Keeping in touch with friends and family
- Planning and prioritising each day's activities
- Taking your full holiday entitlement
- Planning changes in your life on a staged basis whenever possible
- Setting your targets in life and then aiming slightly lower – in other words, being realistic
- Talking about your problems – bottling them up creates tension
- Learning relaxation techniques
- Having fun

# Words of Wisdom

Courage is fear that has said its prayers.

If at first you don't succeed, you'll get a lot of advice.

A woman was describing her husband to a friend: 'He's the kind of man who always hits the nail right on the thumb.'

An expert is a man who will know tomorrow why the things he predicted yesterday didn't happen today.

If you don't think there is strength in numbers, consider the fragile snowflake. If enough of them stick together, they can paralyse a city.

It might be just as offensive to be around a man who never changes his mind as one who never changes his clothes

.

> 'I sit on a man's back assuring him that I will
> do everything possible to alleviate his lot,
> except get off his back.'
>
> – *Leo Tolstoy*

The trouble with many Christians is that they want to reach the promised land without going through the wilderness.

# One Solitary Life

He was born in an obscure village, the child of a peasant woman. He grew up in another village, where he worked in a carpenter shop until he was thirty. For three years he was an itinerant preacher. He never wrote a book. He never held an office. He never had a family or owned a house. He didn't go to college. He never visited a big city. He never travelled 200 miles from the place where he was born. He did none of the things one usually associates with greatness.

He had no credentials but himself. He was only thirty-three when the tide of public opinion turned against him. His friends ran away. He was turned over to his enemies and went through a mockery of a trial. He was nailed to a cross between two thieves. While he was dying, his executioners gambled for his clothing, the only property he had on earth. When he was dead, he was laid in a borrowed grave through the pity of a friend.

Nineteen centuries have come and gone, and today he is the central figure of the human race and the leader of humankind's progress.

All the armies that ever marched, all the navies that ever sailed, all the parliaments that ever sat, all the kings that ever reigned, put together, have not affected the life of man on this earth as much as that One Solitary Life.

# The Gift of Happiness

Learning to live joyfully is a formidable challenge. We are all trying to learn this difficult art, and some of us are better at it than others. Cardinal Newman once wrote, 'I do not fear that I may have to die. I fear that I have never lived.'

The resurrection of Jesus lights our path, as does the promise of eternal life.

We should be happy, render others happy and not wait for a better world. We should be grateful for every moment in life.

Is it possible to take such advice seriously? Can we simply decide to be happy? There are some who find the idea absurd. There is so much suffering in the world that we could question whether one even has the right to pursue the goal of happiness. Yet God made us for happiness.

God waits patiently for us to understand that happiness is possible, even in the midst of pain and sorrow. Parallel to the river of sorrow flows the river of joy.

Translating this level of faith into action takes effort and imagination, but it can be done. Here are some ideas to help you on our spiritual journey:

- Look at the people you meet today with gratitude in your heart. Each of them is God's child and we are called to love them.

- Be grateful to God for all the food you eat today.

- Take the initiative and make one phone call or write one letter today as a way of telling someone that you care.

- Practise some kindness today; smile more often than usual.

- Give a compliment today; point out the good in others.

- Forgive those who have offended you.

- If you want to understand God's gift of happiness and joy, you must first believe in him, not the other way around.

- Believe deeply and, in a leap of faith, joy will surely come to you.

# The Paradox

..........................................

He was born
But he was already begotten.
He issued from a woman
But she was a virgin.
He was wrapped in swaddling clothes
But he removed the swaddling clothes at
     the grave
when he rose again.
He was baptised as man
But he forgave sins as God.
He hungered
But he fed thousands.
He thirsted
But he cried; 'if any man thirsts, let him
     come to me and drink.'
He was weary
But he is the peace of those who are
     sorrowful and heavy-laden.
He weeps
But he put an end to tears.
He is bruised and wounded
But he heals every disease and every
     infirmity.
He is lifted up and nailed to a tree
But by the tree of life, he restores us.
He lays down his life
But he has power to take it again.

He dies

But he gives life and, by his death, destroys
  death.

He is buried

But he rises again.

*Walter Scott and Francis De Sales*

# Pearls of Wisdom

Smart people speak from experience. Smarter people, from experience, don't speak.

Language is a wonderful thing. It can be used to express our thoughts, to conceal our thoughts, or to replace thinking.

'Affection can withstand very severe storms
and turbulence but not a long polar frost of
indifference.'

*– Walter Scott*

Nothing is so strong as gentleness; nothing
so gentle as real strength.

*– St Francis De Sales*

Success in marriage is much more than finding the right person; it is a matter of being the right person.

Quiet people aren't the only ones who don't say much.

# Mother's Day
# Special

....................

There are those who think Mother's Day is just an American invention to make money on cards, flowers and eating out. Maybe, but if mothers feel wanted and appreciated, then I'm all for it.

I came across a piece in my file recently. It was called 'Mother, I remember'. It was written by a middle-aged nun who is taking of her ailing mother. This is part of what she wrote:

'When I enter the room and the loudness of the TV shocks my senses and irritation surges through me ... I remember those times, Mother, when I was a teenager and you gracefully put up with my radio and stereo at full volume.

When it hurts me to see you fumble to open the milk carton with your arthritic fingers ... I remember those same fingers patiently untying a knot in my shoe-lace.

When I see your eyes growing dim with age ... I remember how those eyes would twinkle with delight at my smallest accomplishments.

When you talk on and on about things and people who are no longer a part of my life ... I remember your patience when I would ask you endless questions and you gently responded to each.

When you walk so slowly that I grow impatient ... I remember the walks we took around the neighbourhood when you would adjust your steps to my small feet.

When my heart skips a beat as you stumble and I quickly reach out to help you ... I remember how you walked by my side, ready to catch me while I learned to ride my bike.

When you jump to conclusions and it drives me wild ... I remember how gently you dealt with my growing pains when I was an adolescent.

And when you seem a million miles away, lost in your own little world ... I remember best of all, when I would snuggle close to you and feel your reassuring arm around me.'

# Fancy Meeting You!

I dreamt death came the other night
and Heaven's gate swung wide.
With kindly grace an angel came
and ushered me inside.
And there to my astonishment
stood folk I'd known on earth.
Some I had judged as quite unfit
or of but little worth.
Indignant words rose to my lips
but never were set free,
For every face showed stunned surprise
– no one expected me!

# Don't Quit

When things go wrong as they sometimes will,
When the road you're trudging seems all uphill,
When the funds are low and the debts are high,
And you want to smile, but you have to sigh,
When care is pressing you down a bit,
Rest if you must, but don't you quit.
Life is queer with its twists and turns,
As every one of us sometimes learns.
And many a failure turns about
When he might have won had he stuck it out;
Don't give up though the pace seems slow –
You may succeed with another blow.
Success is failure inside out –
The silver tint of the clouds of doubt,
And you never can tell just how close you are,
It may be near when it seems so far;
So stick to the fight when you're hardest hit –
It's when things seem worst that you must not quit.

# A Few More Words of Wisdom

...............................

The people to worry about are not those who openly disagree with you, but those who disagree and are too cowardly to let you know.

There may be two sides to every question, but there are also two sides to a sheet of fly paper, and it makes a big difference to the fly which side he chooses.

If legs were a new invention, we would realise that they are more remarkable than the car or even the wheel.

Good people learn to break big problems into small ones. In one of Aesop's fables, a farmer asked his sons to gather a bundle of sticks. The farmer tied them together with a strong cord. 'Break the bundle,' he told each of them. But they could not do so. 'Now, untie the bundle and break each stick separately,' he said. That worked.

There are two kinds of failure – the man who will do nothing that he is told and the man who will do nothing else.

The practical man is the man who knows how to get what he wants. The philosopher is the man who knows what man ought to want. The ideal man is the man who knows how to get what he ought to want.

# A Heavenly Round
# of Golf

Once there was a man who was such a golf addict that he was neglecting his job. Frequently he would call in sick as an excuse to play.

One morning, after making his usual call to the office, an angel spotted him on the way to the golf course and decided to teach him a lesson. 'If you play golf today, you will be punished,' the angel whispered in the man's ear.

Thinking it was only his conscience, which he had successfully whipped in the past, the man just smiled .

'No,' he said, 'I've been doing this for years. No one will ever know. I won't be punished.'

The angel said no more and the man stepped up to the first tee where he promptly whacked the ball 300 yards straight down the middle of the fairway. Since he had never driven the ball more than 200 yards, he couldn't believe it. Yet, there it was.

And his luck continued. Long drives on every hole, perfect putting. By the ninth hole he was six under par and was playing near-perfect golf. The fellow was walking on air.

He wound up with an amazing 61, about 30 strokes under his usual game. Wait until he got back to the office to tell them about this! But suddenly, his face fell. He couldn't tell them. He could never tell anyone.

The angel smiled.

# Beware of this Inner Peace!

Be on the lookout for symptoms of inner peace: it is possible that people everywhere could come down with it in epidemic proportions. This could pose a serious threat to what has been, up to now, a fairly stable condition of conflict in the world.

Ten signs and symptoms of inner peace:

1. A tendency to think and act spontaneously rather than on fears based on past experiences.
2. An unmistakable ability to enjoy each moment.
3. Loss of interest in judging other people.
4. Loss of interest in conflict.
5. Loss of ability to worry (a very serious symptom).
6. Frequent overwhelming episodes of appreciation.
7. Contented feeling of connectedness with others and with nature.
8. Frequent attacks of smiling.
9. An increased tendency to let things happen rather than make them happen.
10. Increased susceptibility to the love extended by others as well as the uncontrollable urge to love them back.

# A Wise King

In ancient times an Irish king was asked how he had achieved his station in life. He said:

> I was a listener in the woods.
> I was a gazer at the stars.
> I was blind where secrets were concerned.
> I was silent in wilderness.
> I was talkative among many.
> I was mild in the mead-hall.
> I was stern in battle.
> I was gentle towards allies.
> I was a physician of the sick.
> I was weak towards the feeble.
> I was strong towards the powerful.
> I did not deride the old though I was
>     young.
> I would not speak of anyone in his
>     absence.
> I would not reproach but I would praise.
> I would not ask but I would give.
> For it is through these habits that the
>     young become old and kingly warriors.

# Answers, Please!

One of my favourite writers is Frederick Buechner. His books are delightful, different and insightful. He's credited with asking the following five questions. And if we could find the answer to these, our vision of life would be clearer.

1. If you had to bet everything you have on whether there is a God or whether there isn't, which side would get your money and why?

2. When you look at your face in the mirror, what do you see in it that you most like and what do you see in it that you most deplore?

3. If you had only one last message to leave to the handful of people who are most important to you, what would it be, in twenty-five words or less?

4. Of all the things you've done in your life, which is the one you'd most like to undo? Which is the one that makes you the happiest to remember?

5. Is there any person in the world or any cause that, if circumstances called for it, you'd be willing to die for?

# The Shape
# That I'm In

There is nothing the matter with me.
I am as healthy as I can be,
I have arthritis in both my knees.
And when I talk, I talk with a wheeze.
My pulse is weak and my blood is thin,
But I'm awfully well for the shape I'm in.
Arch supports I have on my feet,
Or I wouldn't be able to be on the street.
Sleep is denied me, night after night,
But every morning I find I'm all right.
My memory is failing, my head's in a spin,
But I'm awfully well for the shape that I'm in.
The moral is this, as my tale I unfold,
That for you and me who are growing old,
It's better to say, 'I'm fine', with a grin,
Than to let folks know the shape that we're in.
How do I know my youth is all spent,
Well, my get-up-and-go just got up and went.
But I really don't mind when I think with a grin,
Of all the grand places my get-up has been.
Old age is golden, I've heard it said,
But sometimes I wonder as I get into bed.
With my ears in the drawer and my teeth in a cup,
My eyes on the table until I wake up,
E'er sleep overtakes me I say to myself,

Is there anything else I should leave on the shelf?
I get up each morning and dust off my wits,
And pick up the paper and read the obits.
If my name is still missing, I know I'm not dead,
So, I have a good breakfast and go back to bed.

# Remember ...

Hospitality is making your guest feel at home, even though you wish they were.

Don't worry how great your talent is, use what you have.

Consider what would happen if the only birds who sang were the ones who sang the best.

The hammer shatters glass but forges steel.

A conference is a gathering of important people who singly can do nothing, but together can decide that nothing can be done.

'I must do something' will always solve more problems than 'Something must be done'.

# Autobiography in Five Chapters

Some unknown person wrote *An Autobiography in Five Chapters*. Each chapter represents a different attitude.

### Chapter One

I walk down the street.
There is a deep hole in the sidewalk
I fall in.
I am lost ... I am helpless.
It isn't my fault.
It takes forever to find a way out.

### Chapter Two

I walk down the same street.
There is a deep hole in the sidewalk.
I pretend I don't see it.
I fall in again.
I can't believe I'm in the same place.
But it isn't my fault.
It still takes a long time to get out.

### Chapter Three

I walk down the same street,

There is a deep hole in the sidewalk.
I see it is there.
I fall in ... it's a habit ... but my eyes are open.
I know where I am.
It is my fault.
I get out immediately.

## Chapter Four

I walk down the same street,
There is a deep hole in the sidewalk.
I walk around it.

## Chapter Five

I walk down a different street.

# With Apologies to Darwin

.........................

Three monkeys sat in a coconut tree,
Discussing all things as they're said to be.
Said one to the others, 'Now listen, you two,
There's a rumour about that can't be true,
That man's descended from our noble race,
The very idea's a big disgrace!
'No monkey every deserted his wife,
Or starved her babies or ruined their lives,
Or passed them on from one to another,
Till they scarcely know who is their mother.
And another thing you'll never see,
A monkey build a fence round a coconut tree,
Starvation would force you to steal from me.
And another thing also a monkey won't do,
Is go out for the night and get on the stew.
Or use a gun, or a club, or a knife,
To take some other poor monkey's life.
'Yes, man descended with lots of fuss,
But brother, he didn't descend from us!'

# After a While You
# Learn

................

After a while you learn
the subtle difference
between holding a hand
and chaining a soul.
And you learn
that love does not mean leaning,
and company does not mean security.
And you begin to learn
that kisses are not contracts,
and presents are not promises.
And you begin to accept your defeats
with your head up and your eyes ahead,
with the grace of a woman or a man,
with the grief of a child.
And you learn to build all your roads on today,
because tomorrow's ground
is too uncertain for plans,
and futures have a way of falling down
in mid-flight.
After a while you learn
that even sunshine burns if you ask too much.
So you plant your own garden
and decorate your own soul
instead of waiting for someone to bring
    flowers.

And you learn
that you really can endure,
that you really are strong,
and you really do have worth.
And you learn,
and you learn,
with every goodbye
you learn ...

◇◇◇◇◇◇◇◇◇◇◇◇◇◇◇◇◇◇◇◇◇◇◇◇◇◇◇◇◇◇◇◇◇◇◇◇◇◇◇◇◇◇◇◇◇◇◇◇◇◇◇◇◇◇◇◇◇◇

# The Best Things in
# Life are Free

Money will buy ...
A bed but not sleep
Books but not brains
Food but not appetite
Medicine but not health
Fashion but not beauty
Amusement but not happiness
A house but not a home.
It really is true that the
Best things in life are free.

# I Am Living

Just to say that I am living
– I am not among the dead
Though I'm getting more forgetful
and confused inside my head.
I've got used to my arthritis
– to my dentures I'm resigned,
I can cope with my bifocals
– but I miss my mind!
Sometimes I can't remember,
when I'm standing by the stair,
Am I going up for something
or have I just come down from there?
It's not my turn to write to you,
I hope you won't feel sore.
I think that I have written
and don't wish to be a bore.
So remember that I miss you
and wish that you were near
And now it's time to post this,
and say goodbye old dear.
Now I stand before the postbox,
my face is really red:
Instead of posting this to you
– I opened it instead!
Love from – oh, this really is a shame:
I went to write my signature
– and forgot my bloomin' name!

# Risk It

To laugh is to risk appearing the fool.
To weep is to risk appearing sentimental.
To reach out to another is to risk
    involvement.
To express feelings is to risk expecting
    your true self.
To place your ideas, your dreams, before
    the crowd,
is to risk their loss.
To love is to risk not being loved in return.
To live is to risk dying.
To hope is to risk despair.
To try is to risk failure.
But risks must be taken,
Because the greatest hazard in life is to risk
    nothing.
The person who risks nothing, does
    nothing,
has nothing, and is nothing.
He may avoid suffering and sorrow,
but he simply cannot learn, feel, change,
    grow, love, live.
Only a person who risks is free.

# Thank You

I love you
not only for what you are,
but for what I am when I am with you.
I love you
not only for what you have made of
    yourself,
but for what you are making of me.
I love you
for the part of me that you bring out;
for passing over the many foolish and
    weak things
you find in me
and for drawing out into the light
all the beautiful things only you could find
    in me.
You have done more for me than any
    creed.
You have made me feel my own goodness.
And all this you have done
with your touch,
with your words,
with yourself.
Thank you.

# Spot On!

If you can start your day without caffeine,
If you can get along without pep pills,
If you can always be cheerful ignoring
    aches and pains,
If you can resist complaining and boring
    people with your troubles,
If you can eat the same food every day and
    be grateful for it,
If you can understand when your loved
    ones are too busy
    to give you any time,
If you can forgive your friends for their
    lack of consideration,
If you can overlook it when those you
    love take it out on you when through
    no fault of your own something goes
    wrong,
If you can take criticism and blame
    without resentment,
If you can ignore a friend's limited
    education and never correct him,
If you can face the world without lies and
    deceit.
If you can conquer tensions without
    medical help,
If you can relax without alcohol,

If you can sleep without the aid of drugs,
If you can honestly say that deep in your
heart you have no prejudice against
creed or colour, religion or politics,
Then, my friend, you're almost as good ...
as your dog!

# Notice

THIS OFFICE REQUIRES NO PHYSICAL
FITNESS PROGRAMME!

Everyone gets enough exercise
jumping to conclusions,
flying off the handle,
running down the boss,
knifing friends in the back,
dodging responsibility,
passing the buck
and pushing their luck.

# Tell Me Now

If with pleasure you are viewing
Any work that I am doing,
If you like me or you love me,
Tell me now.
Don't withhold your approbation,
Till the Father makes oration,
And I lie with snowy lilies o'er my brow.
For no matter how you shout it,
I won't care much about it;
I won't see how many teardrops you have shed.
If you think some praise is due me,
Now's the time to slip it to me,
For I cannot read my tombstone when I'm dead.
More than fame and more than money,
Is the comment warm and sunny,
Is the hearty warm approval of a friend;
For it gives a life a savour,
And it makes me stronger, braver,
And it gives me spirit right up to the end.
If I earn your praise, bestow it,
If you like me, let me know it,
Let the words of true encouragement be said.
Do not wait till life is over
And I'm underneath the clover,
For I cannot read my tombstone when I'm
    dead.

# Difficult Things
# To Do

................

To break a bad habit
To love an enemy
To live logically
To admit ignorance
To withhold judgement
To grow old gracefully
To persevere without haste
To wait without impatience
To suffer without complaint
To know when to keep silent
To be indifferent to ridicule
To concentrate in the midst of strife
To endure hatred without resentment
To fraternise without losing individuality
To serve without compensation,
    commendation or recognition.

# Slow Dance

Have you ever watched children on a
  merry-go-round?
Or listened to the rain slipping on the
  ground?
Ever followed a butterfly's erratic flight?
Or gazed at the sun into the fading light?
You had better slow down; don't dance so
  fast:
Time is short and the music won't last.
Do you run through each day on a fly?
When the day is done do you lie in your bed
With the next hundred chores running
  through your head?
You had better slow down, don't dance so
  fast:
Time is short and the music won't last.
When you run so fast to get somewhere
You lose half the fun of getting there.
When you worry and hurry through your
  day
It is like an unopened gift, thrown away.
Life is not a race. Do take it slower.
Hear the music before the song is over.
You had better slow down, don't dance so
  fast:
Time is short and the music won't last.

# Open-mindedness

Closed-minded people put others down,
Open-minded people are tolerant and
understanding.
Closed-minded people cannot see the good
in people who disagree with them,
Open-minded people see some good in
everyone.
Closed-minded people mind other people's
business,
Open-minded people mind their own.
Closed-minded people are envious and
jealous,
Open-minded people are contented and
thankful.
Closed-minded people know it all,
Open-minded people realise how little we
all know.
Closed-minded people belittle our cultures
and customs,
Open-minded people know the value of diversity.
Closed-minded people are suspicious and
overly cautious,
Open-minded people are trusting and
adventurous.
Closed-minded people talk without
thinking,

Open-minded people think before talking.
Closed-minded people think they are
    always right,
Open-minded people realise how easy it is
    to be wrong.
Closed-minded people like to judge others,
Open-minded people let others judge them.

# Everybody – Somebody – Anybody – Nobody

There was an important job to be done.
**Everybody** was asked to do it.
**Everybody** was sure that **Somebody**
    would do it.
**Anybody** could have done it, but in the
    end **Nobody** did it.
**Somebody** got very angry about that
    because it was **Everybody**'s job.
**Everybody** thought **Anybody** would do
    it.
But **Nobody** realised that **Everybody**
    wouldn't do it.
It ended up that **Everybody** blamed
    **Somebody** when actually **Nobody** had
    asked **Anybody**.

# Ten Commandments
# For Good Human
# Relations

1.  Speak to people. There is nothing as nice as a cheerful word or greeting.

2.  Smile at people. It takes seventy-two muscles to frown, only fourteen to smile.

3.  Call people by name. The sweetest music to anyone's ears is the sound of their name.

4.  Be friendly and helpful. If you want friends, be friendly.

5.  Be cordial. Speak and act as if everything you do is a genuine pleasure.

6.  Be genuinely interested in people. Everyone has something likeable in them if you look for it.

7.  Be generous with praise but cautious with criticism.

8.  Be considerate of the feelings of others – it will be appreciated.

9.  Be thoughtful of the opinions of others. There are three sides to every controversy – yours, the others person's and the right one.

10. Be alert to give help; what counts in life is what we do for others.

# The Tate Family

Let me introduce you to the Tate Family. They are a big and very influential family, present in every parish and community group.

- First there is **Dictate**, who wants to run everything and usually does until there's nothing left to run.
- Then you'll find that **Rotate** will come in to try to change everything.
- But he will be blocked by **Irritate**, who stirs up plenty of trouble with the help of his friend **Agitate.**
- Whenever there are changes to be made and new projects to get off the ground **Hesitate** and **Vegetate** want to wait until next year or a more suitable time – which usually means some time when they won't have to change at all.
- Very prominent in every community is **Imitate**, who wants everything to be run exactly the way he runs it.
- But the one that really upsets him is **Devastate**, who provides the voice of doom.
- Then there is **Facilitate**, who is most helpful when there is work to be done. In fact, she is the one who keeps the whole community going, always trying to keep the peace when everyone else is losing their head.
- There is always a battle between **Cogitate** and **Meditate** as to which of them will think things over

more. Both of them are introspective and both of them think themselves wiser than they actually are.

- Finally, there's a member of the Tate Family that nobody wants to talk about, the black sheep. He's **Amputate**, who has cut himself off completely from the rest of the family.

The question we have to ask ourselves is this: Which of the Tates are we? Or perhaps at different times in our lives are we all of the Tates?

# The Devil's Beatitudes

Blessed are those who are too tired, too busy, too distracted, to spend an hour once a week with fellow Christians in the church – they are my best workers.

Blessed are those Christians who wait to be asked and expect to be thanked – I can use them.

Blessed are the touchy: with a bit of luck they may stop going to church – they are my missionaries.

Blessed are the troublemakers – they shall be called my children.

Blessed are those who have no time to pray – they are easy prey to me.

Blessed are the complainers – I'm all ears for them.

Blessed are you when you read this and think it is about other people and not yourself – I've got you!

# Tomorrow

He was going to be all that a mortal could
    be – Tomorrow.
No one would be kinder or braver than he
    – Tomorrow.
A friend who was troubled and weary he knew
Who'd be glad of a lift and need it too:
On him he would call and see what he
    could do –Tomorrow.
Each morning he stacked up the letters
    he'd write – Tomorrow.
And he thought of the folks he would fill
    with delight – Tomorrow
It was too bad, indeed, he was busy today,
And hadn't a minute to stop on his way,
'More time I'll have to give others', he'd
    say – Tomorrow.
The greatest of workers this man would
    have been – Tomorrow.
The world would have known him had he
    ever seen – Tomorrow.
But the fact is he died, and he faded from
    view,
And all that he left here when living was
    through
Was a mountain of things he intended to
    do –Tomorrow.

# A Good Marriage

A good marriage must be created.
In marriage the little things are the big
    things.
It is never being too old to hold hands.
It is remembering to say, 'I love you'. At
    least once a day.
It is never going to sleep angry.
It is having a mutual sense of values and
    common objectives.
It is standing together to face the world.
It is forming a circle of love that gathers in
    the whole family.
It is speaking words of appreciation and
    demonstrating gratitude in thoughtful
    ways.
It is having the capacity to forgive and
    forget.
It is giving each other an atmosphere in
    which each can grow.
It is not only marrying the right person.
It is being the right partner.

# Rules for a Happy Marriage

1. Never be angry at the same time.
2. Never yell at each other unless the house is on fire.
3. If one of you has to win an argument let it be the other one.
4. If you have to criticise, do it lovingly.
5. Never bring up mistakes of the past.
6. Neglect the whole world rather than one another.
7. Never go to sleep with an argument unsettled.
8. When you have done something wrong, be ready to admit it and ask for forgiveness.
9. At least once every day, try to say one kind, complimentary thing to your partner.

# Children Learn
# What They Live
# With

If children live with criticism, they learn to
condemn.

If they live with hostility, they learn to
fight.

If they live with ridicule, they learn to be
shy.

If they live with shame, they learn to feel
guilty.

If they live with tolerance, they learn to be
patient.

If they live with encouragement, they learn
to have confidence.

If they live with praise, they learn to
appreciate.

If they live with fairness, they learn what
justice is.

If they live with security, they learn to
trust.

If they live with approval, they learn to
like themselves.

If they live with acceptance and friendship,
they learn to find love and God in the
world.

# Take Time

Take time to THINK:
It is the source of power.
Take time to PLAY:
It is the secret of perpetual youth.
Take time to READ:
It is the fountain of wisdom.
Take time to PRAY:
It is the greatest power on earth.
Take time to LOVE and BE LOVED:
It is a God-given privilege.
Take time to be FRIENDLY:
It is the road to happiness.
Take time to LAUGH:
It is the music of the soul.
Take time to GIVE:
It is too short a day to be selfish.
Take time to WORK:
It is the price of success.
Take time to do CHARITY:
It is the key to heaven.

# Success

Success is speaking words of praise,
in cheering other people's ways,
in doing just the best you can,
with every task and every plan.
It's silence when your speech would hurt,
politeness when your neighbour's curt.
It's deafness when the scandal flows
and sympathy with other's woes.
It's loyalty when duty calls.
It's courage when disaster falls.
It's patience when the hours are long.

# Happiness

Half the happiness of living
Comes from willing-hearted giving;
Comes from sharing all our pleasures,
From dividing all our treasures.
And the other half is loving,
First the Lord, then all things living.
So, each mortal should be sowing
Love seeds while his life is growing,
For all happiness in living
Comes from loving and from giving.

# A Special Person

God made every one of us
Then put us down on earth,
To see how we would make out
and how we'd show our worth.
He examines us occasionally
and looks at what we do,
Our kindness and our honesty,
So he must be pleased with you.
You do your best for everyone
You're there if they should fall,
And another thing about you,
You seldom judge at all.
He's probably looking down
And he's bound to feel quite proud.
It's a cert he'll spot you right away,
you stand out in the crowd.

# What a Jigsaw Puzzle Can Teach Us About Life

Don't force a fit. If something is meant to be, it will come together naturally.

When things aren't going so well, take a break. Everything will look different when you return.

Be sure to look at the big picture. Getting hung up on the little pieces only leads to frustration.

Perseverance pays off. Every important puzzle went together bit by bit, piece by piece.

When one spot stops working, move to another. But be sure to come back later.

The creator of the puzzle gave you the picture as a guidebook.

Variety is the spice of life. It's the different colours and patterns that make the puzzle interesting.

Establish the border first. Boundaries give a sense of security and order.

Don't be afraid to try different combinations. Some matches are surprising.

Take time to celebrate your successes (even little ones).

Anything worth doing takes time and effort. A great puzzle can't be rushed.

# The Power of Words

In the Bee Gees' hit 'Words' was the famous line, 'It's only words, and words are all I have to take your heart away.'

Words are our primary way of communicating. They are powerful tools for good or for bad. William Ward once said, 'Our words can cut or comfort, hinder or help, harass or heal, injure or inspire ... each time we speak we deliver our own state-of-the-heart address.

Encouraging words give us a lift.

On the other hand, verbal abuse kills the spirit. Words spoken in anger, guilt or resentment cut to the quick. There was a song here in Ireland with the philosophical title, 'Whatever you say, say nothing'. And if your words don't build up and encourage, it surely is better to say nothing.

# Things You Can Learn From a Dog

- Allow the experience of fresh air and the wind in your face to be pure ecstasy.
- When loved ones come home, always run to greet them.
- When it's in your best interest, practise obedience.
- Let others know when they've invaded your territory.
- Take naps and stretch before rising.
- Run, romp and play daily.
- Eat with gusto and enthusiasm.
- Be loyal.
- Never pretend to be something you're not.
- If what you want lies buried, dig until you find it.
- When someone is having a bad day, be silent, sit close by, nuzzle them gently.
- Thrive on attention and let people touch you.
- Avoid biting when a simple growl will do.
- On hot days, drink lots of water and lie under a shady tree.
- When you're happy, dance around and wag your entire body.
- No matter how often you're scolded, don't buy into guilt and pout ... run right back and make friends.
- Bond with your pack.
- Delight in the simple joy of a long walk.

# True Prophets

Martin Luther King said: 'We are supposed to be Good Samaritans helping the afflicted on the road to Jericho, but it is even more important to make sure that the road to Jericho is transformed so the men and women will not be constantly robbed as they make their journey on life's highway.'

'True compassion is more than flinging a coin to a beggar. True compassion sees that the edifice which produces beggars is restructured!'

True prophets make us uncomfortable. And Martin Luther King was a prophet who pulled no punches. That is why he was assassinated.

# Stone Houses

People in the township lived in rows of poorly construct-ed tin houses. They were hammered together in groups so that it wasn't clear where one family ended and the next family began. The conditions were poor yet each family became part of an even bigger family. Everybody shared too. In those conditions there is no mine and thine, but only ours.

In the well-off parts of the township, stone houses were built and very quickly doors were put on the houses and locks put on the doors. That's when the world of mine and thine began.

Perhaps the reason we in the west are so possessive is because the only world we know is the world of stone houses. There's nothing we can do about it – we are not going to live in communal henhouses again – but we must also realise that the world of stone houses soon produces rooms with doors and doors with locks, and not only does one family not share with the next family, even members of the same family don't share. Unlike some of our friends in Africa, we have every material possession, so much so that the possessions now possess us.

# The Stability of a Three-legged Stool

I was enthused by an essay on leadership that I read recently. The writer compared leadership to a three-legged stool. Three-legged stools never rock. Vital if you are trying to squeeze milk from a reluctant cow.

Good leadership is dependent on three legs or sources.

The first leg starts with the desire to be a leader, and examines our gifts, talents, drive and interests. Have we a passion, an imagination and a vision that won't go away? In religious terms we might call it a vocation. In secular terms we ask: 'Are you suited to the job?'

The second source of authority is from above. Who authorises me to be a leader? Who employs me? What manager gave me the job? Have I the authority from the institution?

The third source is from below. Those who are to be led must be willing to be led. They have to agree not to undermine the authority of the leader. If we want to be led we must sacrifice some of our own self-interest and this becomes easier if the leader inspires confidence.

The difficulty is that some leaders have only one source of authority, and collapse immediately. Others can get by with apparent effectiveness on two sources of leadership. But it won't last either.

# Happiness

Psychologists say we can make life easier for ourselves and others by following a few simple guidelines on happiness:

Learn to count your blessings. Once a week take time to write down three or four things that make you happy. They could be small things like seeing a flower bloom or big things like seeing your child take her first steps.

Virtue and vice become easier with practice. Acts of kindness not only help us to be kind but help others too. Let somebody go ahead of you in the queue at the supermarket or coming out of a side road in traffic. Prepare lunch for an old person who wouldn't otherwise get one. Recognising that we can help to others boosts our own happiness.

Enjoy the pleasures of life. If you get a delightful dinner today, enjoy every morsel of it. Take mental pictures of pleasurable moments and play them over in your mind. Gratitude is a way of boosting your happiness. If somebody has helped you, tell them so. Don't wait until they're dead. Brighten that person's life now.

Learn to forgive. Somebody once told me that holding on to resentment is like taking poison yourself and waiting for your enemy to die.

Make time for special people in your life like family and friends.

Strong personal relationships are the best antidote to loneliness. We have to invest time in relationships.

Take care of yourself. It's good to get sleep, exercise, food and rest.

Have personal mental strategies to help you cope with stress.

Little phrases like: 'That which doesn't kill me makes me stronger'; or Roy Keane's famous one: 'If you fail to prepare, you prepare to fail', are helpful. Obviously, for me, religious faith helps me through the difficult times of life.

And, finally, here's one I've told you before but it bears repeating: 'Each of us will have to answer to God for the permissible pleasures in life that we failed to enjoy.' Now when was the last time a preacher told you that pleasure wasn't a sin?

# Spreading the
# Good News

Spreading the Good News is part of every Christian's life. Here are twenty suggestions:

1. Brighten up. Put your biggest worry in God's hands.
2. Read a child a story about the first Christmas or the first Easter.
3. Thank people who have helped you on your faith journey. Tell them what they said or did which affected you.
4. How has God gifted you? Use that talent to make a difference to somebody's life.
5. Be generous to your community. Share your time, skills, money or possessions.
6. Have a look at how you work. Be more just and life-giving.
7. Explain to a friend the reasons you believe.
8. Thank somebody who has a tedious job, for example the car park attendant, the person at the checkout, the cashier in the restaurant.
9. Look at the subtle ways you keep somebody dependent and powerless. How can you change, to affirm that person's worth?
10. Count your blessings and then tell them to someone else.

11. Say thanks to a suffering person for the way they have persevered in hope and for the special witness they offer you.

12. Make up for the back-biting spiral that goes on by affirming other people's qualities in your own conversation as often as possible.

13. Romance your spouse, girlfriend or boyfriend in a special way.

14. Give up a destructive habit, for example running yourself down, and replace it with a positive one, such as affirmation of self.

15. Listen – really listen to someone you thought you knew already. Discover yet another God-given uniqueness about him or her and say what it is.

16. Think what a great gift faith is. Let go of a long-standing grudge.

17. Put yourself in another's shoes. Work hard at overcoming a deeply ingrained prejudice.

18. Contemplate the gift of health and make the most of it.

19. Be pro-life by praising a parent, welcoming a child or offering help to a pregnant mum or an expectant dad.

20. Last, but not least, try thanking a tired priest.

# Living the Message

On Sunday morning he is sitting in church with his family. On Monday morning he and his partners are making promises to customers they know they can never keep. He gets the contracts but doesn't see the contradiction between Sunday and Monday in his life.

She's a member of the choir. After singing God's praises she and her friends meet for lunch and tear another choir member's character to pieces. The Jesus she serves in praise and song is betrayed over a bottle of white wine and a salad.

We know the Creed by heart and wouldn't think of missing Mass. But we walk by the homeless person with the outstretched hand, without ever noticing him.

# The Deadly Sins

According to the BBC the seven deadly sins are out of date. To save your embarrassment, the seven deadly sins as of old were these: Anger, pride, envy, gluttony, lust, sloth and greed.

According to the *Heaven and Earth* show survey, very few people think that is a list of sins at all. Only 9 per cent said they had been guilty of committing any of those sins. They must be saints. Of those who admitted giving in to one of the deadly sins, 79 per cent gave way to anger, followed by pride, envy, lust and sloth, while only 54 per cent admitted to the sin of greed.

Not unexpectedly, lust was the sin that both men and women said they would enjoy most. Surprisingly, gluttony was a popular sin with women, but not with men.

Now we're more concerned with actions that hurt other people, rather than the seven deadly sins.

The new list of deadly sins according to the people asked in this survey are: cruelty, hypocrisy, selfishness, greed,. dishonesty, bigotry and adultery. You'll notice that greed is on both the old and new lists. In fact, it could be argued that the new list is really the same list with a different emphasis. By any standard there's a close connection between lust and adultery. And there's strong case to be made that the basis of all sin is selfishness. What I'm delighted about is that people still think sin exists.

I wonder what your list would be? But before you start writing, remember that as soon as you point a finger at anybody else, three fingers point back at yourself.

# Learn From Your Mistakes

We all burn energy making martyrs of ourselves. Worse still are the 'if only' brigade. It's as simple as this. What has happened can't be undone. So don't make things worse by throwing a good life after a bad one. There's not a person on earth who doesn't wish that they had lived life differently. But there's no point doing your head in fighting against reality. Make up your mind to let things go. That way you give yourself permission to have a fresh start.

Don't make the same mistakes over and over again. If something goes wrong think about it, spot where it went wrong, then take some action to ensure it doesn't go wrong next time. If you have made a mess of things and said something stupid to another person, don't let it simmer. Say sorry, admit your mistake, it won't kill you: When you are up front about it you can leave your mistakes behind you. It's not the mistake that is the problem but how you handle it.

# Be Grateful

Those who are grateful for their gifts are always more positive than those who spend their lives complaining about gifts they don't have. Take time to think about what you have and be grateful for it.

Like yourself. It seems obvious when you say it. If you don't like yourself, why should anybody else like you? There will be things about yourself that you don't like. Change them. Don't use them as an excuse to hate yourself. I have always found it useful to list five gifts and then try to prioritise them.

Another tip is to do something enjoyable every day. If you keep putting off what you enjoy, then you will never find time for it.

Likewise, if you have a list of problems, try and sort at least one of them today.

Make the most of your opportunities and never stop working on yourself to be better.

# Take a Break From the Rat Race

A friend offers seven easy steps to ease away tension:
1. Do nothing.
2. Laugh out loud. Enjoy jokes.
3. Tune into soothing music.
4. Think happy. Imagine a loved one or a peaceful scene.
5. Take a ten-minute walk.
6. Inhale and exhale for five seconds on each breath.
7. Take a few moments to tense and relax your muscles from head to toe.

# Recognise Yourself?

We are appalled by and ashamed of what Judas did, but most of us have a few secret pieces of silver in our pocket. Could the reason we show no compassion to people who betray us be that we can recognise the Judas chromosome within ourselves?

And before we judge Peter too harshly, remember the sound of the rooster crowing when our silence betrays someone.

When we disconnect the value of the gospel from the reality of our lives, Judas and Peter take over.

# Use Your Time Well

Make good use of your time by doing good for others and by helping others to do good themselves. It's sound advice and, if we want, we can always find time. Here are ten simple things each of us could do that would take up no time at all:

1. Make a conscious effort to smile.
2. Say 'Please', 'Thank you', 'Excuse me'.
3. Give a sincere compliment where it is deserved.
4. Remember someone's name and how to pronounce it.
5. Hold the door open for the person behind you.
6. Let someone go ahead of you at the supermarket checkout.
7. Leave a bigger tip than you normally would to somebody who deserves it.
8. Bring a cup of tea or coffee to a colleague.
9. Say 'Good morning' to your co-workers.
10. Do a message for a sick neighbour while you are doing your own.

# Moses Maimonides

I came across a piece written in the twelfth century by the Jewish philosopher Moses Maimonides. He said that there are eight degrees of charity.

1.  The first and the lowest degree is to give, but with reluctance and regret. A gift of the hand but not of the heart.

2.  The second is to give cheerfully but not proportionately to the distress of the suffering.

3.  The third is to give cheerfully and proportionately but not until we are solicited.

4.  The fourth is to give cheerfully, proportionately and even when unsolicited, but to put it in the poor man's hand, thereby causing him the painful emotion of shame.

5.  The fifth is to give charity in such a way that the distressed may receive the bounty and know their benefactor without being known to him. Such was the conduct of some of our ancestors who used to tie up money in the back pocket of their cloaks so that the poor might take it unnoticed.

6.  The sixth, which rises still higher, is to know the object of our bounty but remain unknown to them. Such was the conduct of those of our ancestors who used to convey their charitable gifts into the

poor people's dwellings, taking care that their own persons and names should remain unknown.

7. The seventh is better still, namely to give charity in such a way that the giver may not know the relieved persons, nor they the name of the giver.

8. The best way of all is to anticipate charity by preventing poverty; namely to assist needy brothers or sisters either by a considerable gift or a loan of money, or by teaching them a trade or by putting them in the way of business, so that they may earn an honest livelihood and not be forced to the dreadful alternative of holding out their hands for charity. This is the highest step and the best charity of all.

# All are Welcome

Jesus was at pains to point out that all genuine people are welcome in his community. He invited all people of good will to communion. He would not refuse communion to those who struggle with imperfection. He would not reject those in loving relationships. He would not humiliate anyone looking for his help.

No matter how tired we've become, we cannot allow heartless tyrants to hijack either our loving God or our beloved church.

We have to stand against those who make God ridiculous and irrelevant. We must do it for God's sake.

# God is
# Non-exclusive

The God I believe in is a God who excludes no one. He brought people to a banquet and those who didn't want to go were cast aside. It was open to everyone on the highways and byways – no one was excluded.

God is a God who welcomed the prodigal son home, saw him from a long way off and was always looking for him. He never listened to a list of sins, but was so glad to see a reconciled heart that he threw a party in his honour. The elder son was miserable about it all. But God had a place in his heart for both of them and he loved both of them. It makes no difference how many times we make mistakes, God always finds something to love in us.

God had ninety-nine sheep safe and sound, but wasn't content until he left them all and went out to look for one stray. Nothing is impossible with our God.

God is a God who paid the workers their just wage when they came to work in the vineyard all day, but also gave those who came in the evening the same amount of money. He was making the point that we don't earn it, and God will be generous anyway.

God is a God who made 180 gallons of wine when a few bottles would have done. Nobody can cork God's generosity. There is more than enough for everyone in God's plan.

God is a God who washed feet. He is a servant God.

God even gave us a final exam in case we'd fail it. 'As

long as you do it to the least of my brethren you do it to me.' God is a God who asked only one question of Peter or any of the apostles who abandoned him. The simple question was this, 'Do you love me?' And when they said yes, God loved them in return.

God is a God who died on the cross. He died on a cross with his arms opened wide in love and acceptance. And they are frozen like that for all eternity. By his wounds we are healed.

# Well Said

Wilfrid Funk, famous for the dictionaries he composed, once listed the most expressive words in the English language:

1. The most bitter word is 'alone'.
2. The most reverend is 'mother'.
3. The most tragic is 'death'.
4. The most beautiful is 'love'.
5. The most peaceful is 'tranquil'.
6. The saddest is 'forgotten'.
7. The warmest is 'friendship'.
8. The coldest is 'no'.
9. The most comforting is 'faith'.

# A Remarkable
# Obituary

........................

Today we mourn the passing of a beloved old friend, Mr Common Sense. Mr Sense had been with us for many years.

He will be remembered as having cultivated such valuable lessons as knowing when to come in out of the rain, why the early bird gets the worm and that life isn't always fair. Common Sense lived by simple, sound financial policies (don't spend more than you earn) and reliable parenting strategies (adults, not kids, are in charge)

His health began to rapidly deteriorate when schools were required to get parental consent to administer aspirin to a student, but could not inform the parents when a student became pregnant and wanted to have an abortion.

Finally, Common Sense lost the will to live as the Ten Commandments became contraband; churches became businesses; and criminals received better treatment than their victims. Common Sense was preceded in death by his parents, Truth and Trust, his wife, Discretion, his daughter, Responsibility, and his son, Reason. Two stepbrothers, My Rights and Ima Whiner, survive him.

Not many attended his funeral because so few realised he was gone.

# A Lifetime

It takes a lifetime to learn to live
How to share and how to give
How to face tragedy that comes your way
How to find courage to face each new day
How to smile when your heart is sore
How to go on when you can take no more
How to laugh when you want to cry
How to be brave when you say goodbye
How to love when your loss is great
How to forgive when you want to hate
How to be sure that God's really there
How to find him – seek him in prayer.

# God's Work of Art

Vincent Van Gogh said that God always sends us works of art so that we can see ourselves in them, and he went on to say that 'The greatest artist of all is Christ, who doesn't work with canvas but rather with human flesh.'

Now there's a lovely thought – even if my life is a failure, I am still one of God's great works of art.

# Just for Today

Just for today I will try to live through this day only, and not tackle all my problems at once. I can do something for twelve hours that would appall me if I felt I had to keep it up for a lifetime. Just for today I will be happy. Most of us are as happy as we make up our minds to be.

Just for today, I will adjust myself to what is, and not try to adjust everything to my own desires. I will take my 'luck' as it comes, and fit myself to it.

Just for today I will try to strengthen my mind. I will study, I will learn something useful. I will read something that requires effort, thought and concentration.

Just for today I will exercise my soul in three ways: I will do somebody a good turn and not get found out; if anybody knows of it, it will not count. I will do at least two things I don't want to do – just for exercise. I will not show anyone that my feelings are hurt; they may be hurt, but today I will not show it.

Just for today I will be agreeable. I will look as well as I can, dress becomingly, talk low, act courteously, criticise not one bit, not find fault with anything and not try to improve or regulate anybody but myself.

Just for today I will have a programme. I may not follow it exactly, but I will have it. I will save myself from two pests: hurry and indecision.

Just for today I will have a quiet half hour all by myself, and relax. I will try to get a better perspective on my life.

Just for today I will be unafraid. Especially I will not be afraid to enjoy what is beautiful, and to believe that as I give to the world, so the Father will give to me.

# God Helps Those ...

A little girl told her father that her brothers were setting traps to catch birds. She was very upset. So he asked her what she was going to do about it. She said, 'I pray that the traps will not work and the birds will go free.'

'Anything else?' her father asked.

'I pray that God will direct the birds away from the traps,' she answered.

'And is that all you did?' the father teased.

She said, 'When the boys weren't looking, I kicked the traps into the ditch.'

Now there's a little girl who understood prayer. 'God helps those who help themselves.'

I love the prayer used by St Thomas More: 'O God, give me the grace to work for the things I pray for.' Which brings us back to the little girl kicking the traps into the ditch.

# How to be Miserable

If you want to be miserable, here are a few rules that never fail. They will certainly take the joy out of your life and probably destroy anyone you happen to meet along the way.

1. Feel sorry for yourself. It's a perfect place to start. Self-pity is guaranteed to make you miserable.

2. Make a list of things that could go wrong but probably won't. Then start worrying about them. It's amazing what can go wrong if you start looking for trouble.

3. If you want to make your own and others' lives miserable you can do it with one single word. Complain. Find fault with everything. Eventually you will become an expert complainer. And when you do you will find flaws everywhere. Never mind the good points, just concentrate on the negative.

4. Insist on bullying other people so that you can always have your own way. Pretend to listen but don't. Don't cooperate. Don't compromise. Don't give in. And when things get tough, quit. You'll have enough misery to last you a lifetime.

5. Gossip and ridicule. Highlight other people's weaknesses. Tell them to their face how bad they are. Talk behind their backs too. You'll spread misery like a contagious disease.

6. Make a mountain out of a molehill. Over-react to

everything. Emphasise what is worst in your work-place, your surroundings, your family, yourself and the people you have to deal with. Accentuate the negative. Speak in an angry voice. You'll spread so much misery you could become too happy.

7. Be selfish and self-centred. Why be concerned about others? If asked to help say no. Even if not asked, develop the kind of face that says, 'Don't come near me.' Let someone else do it. Misery will be your constant companion.

8. Don't entertain compassion, forgiveness or under-standing. You have much more important things to do. Open the door to such positive thoughts and your misery could disappear.

So don't mess with misery. If you do you could begin to laugh at yourself. And if you do that your misery will crumble. Be warned.

◇◇◇◇◇◇◇◇◇◇◇◇◇◇◇◇◇◇◇◇◇◇◇◇◇◇◇◇◇◇◇◇◇◇◇◇◇◇◇◇◇◇◇◇◇◇◇◇◇◇◇

# Twisting the Truth

We can twist facts to suit ourselves. And we need to be careful about that when we are trying to find out what sort of God we adore.

# The Best Journeys

John McGahern says in *Amongst Women*, 'You can only love what you know.' He went on to say, 'The best journeys in life are always among the familiar.' I think that's wonderful. Essentially it means that our best journeys are not away to somewhere else, but among the familiar territory that we now know. Journeys inwards, in other words. How can we love ourselves if we don't even know ourselves? And how can we know ourselves if we don't reflect upon our lives? How can we love God if we don't know God? Which God is it that we know?

I have spent a lot of my life with people who say they don't believe in God any more. And when you ask them which God they don't believe in, I discover I couldn't believe in it either. They don't believe in the vengeful, frightening, fearsome God of their youth and of their catechism. They haven't made the journey inward. They haven't reflected upon God.

The best journeys are among the familiar and that's when we learn to love and to know ourselves and God.

# The Universal Crime

I wonder what is it that stops us from being heroes? I believe our greatest crime is silence. You could add begrudgery or jealousy too.

Silence is the universal crime of decent people. We are silent in the face of evil because we don't want to get involved, are afraid of being snubbed, or of being rejected. But the silence of the many allows the malice of the few to triumph. It was the silence of the majority of Germans that allowed Hitler and his evil few to exterminate six million Jews. It was the silence of white Americans that allowed the murder of Martin Luther King. It was the silence of the vast majority of priests and bishops that allowed 5 per cent of priests to wreak havoc on the Church and, more evilly, destroy the lives of so many young children. Pilate washing his hands is a good symbol of the cowardice that helps evil to flourish.

# Grieving

I am no expert on grieving, but here are a few suggestions about what not to do.

First of all, don't abandon those in need. A woman said to me recently that when her child was killed, people didn't know what to say, so they either said nothing or talked about everything else under the sun.

I never know when I am being helpful. I have to keep reading signs all the time and I know there are many times when I am not seen as being helpful, simply because I am not saying what the person wants to hear.

I have found that people often come back years later and tell me how I helped them, even though I was totally unaware of it at the time. Usually they say something like this: 'You allowed us to talk about it when we wanted to. You also allowed us to have all our feelings. You assured us we weren't going mad.'

Now how I did that, I don't know, but I am glad I did. I would say that's the core of how to be helpful.

# The Miracle of Nature

It's just an ordinary tree, standing majestically in the valley of the field. From where I sit, I have the unusual experience of looking down on it. In spring it's dressed like a model. Leaves, each one different, make it rounded, full, symmetrical, but imperfect enough to be naturally beautiful.

A few weeks ago it was naked and skeletal. Six weeks on, the leaves will pale to a tired yellow, and then turn a sleepy brown before returning to a bony skeleton in October. The miracle is that it will be magnificent and beautiful in every season.

I've watched it for years now, giving food for thought and food to birds no matter how it looks. It gives me perspective in the troubles of life and priesthood and Church. Life comes and life goes on – yours, mine and nature's. Each of us is a work of art, a canvas coloured uniquely by God as he writes straight on crooked lines; imperfect enough to be beautiful and yet loved for what we are. Sometimes we can learn a lot about the preciousness of life from simple facts of nature. Only recently I learned that if there were no insects, most trees, plants, flowers and fruits would disappear from the planet. Furthermore, insects can thrive without us humans but we would perish without insects.

Did you know that a blink lasts exactly 0.3 seconds? A sneeze can travel at about a hundred miles per hour. All babies are colour blind at birth. The human heart will beat 2.5 billion times during a typical life span. Enamel is the hardest substance in the human body. A person has 2 million sweat glands. And girls have more taste buds than boys.

I don't know what all this has to do with anything. But maybe this little quotation from Vaclav Havel would give you hope for your journey: 'Hope is not the conviction that something will turn out well, but the certainty that something makes sense regardless of how it turns out.'

I like that.

# God is Love

God has to be the centre of the spiritual life. Responsibility and gratitude grow out of a recognition that we owe everything to the God of love. If I really want to know God, I read the gospels. Two stories stand out. In the story of the Prodigal Son the sinner (the son) prepared his list well, but God (the father) didn't want to listen to it. He was looking out for his son's return, saw he was genuine, wrapped his arms around him, forgave him, and ordered a party to celebrate his return. That's the truth.

The second story I remember is the time our first pope, St Peter, sinned by denying Jesus. He was treated with respect, not scorn. Jesus didn't force him or the other vulnerable disciples to crawl. He asked one question only: 'Do you love me?' In the end that's all that matters.

# Who Are You?

In every relationship there are at least six people. Who you think you are; who the other thinks you are; who you really are; who she thinks she is; who you think she is; who she really is.

Whether we like it or not, people grow at a different pace. The danger is that unless there is a constant conversation going on, people will also grow to a different place.

Perhaps the most important word is the word love. That's worth thinking about. Did/does he/she love you? There are many relevant issues about duty, vows, entitlements and indeed compromise. But if mutual love is absent, what's the point of any relationship?

# The Unanswered Prayer

Sometimes, as the song says, 'God's greatest gifts to us are unanswered prayers.'

We are to keep on praying, but we must remember that the purpose of our prayer is not to change God, but to change us. That's a wonderful insight that we might well spend time listening to.

# Unconditional Love

I find that unconditional love is admirable in others but almost impossible to practise myself. And yet the longer I think about it the more I realise that if I am to be anything like what God wants me to be, I have to love unconditionally because that's how God loves me. I don't see God as a control freak or a benign puppeteer either. I can't believe God is someone who manipulates me by jerkily pulling the strings of my life. God leaves us free to be ourselves because we're good people the way he made us. We might fail but he still loves us. We can deny him as Peter did and he'll always give us a fresh start.

No matter how hard it is for me, I have to try to love others in the same forgiving way as God loves me. I am not good at it but I have to try it. A reader dropped me a card that sums up what I'm trying to say:

'Live your life in such a way that those who know you, but don't know God, will come to know God, because they have known you.'

Simply put, but hellishly hard to live by.

# Imperfection

Imperfection will always be part of the human condition and, since the Church is peopled by humans, all churches have as many imperfections as gifts.

I should not expect any institution, least of all the Church, to run smoothly. I should remember the lesson of the gospel. In a field of wheat, cockles and weeds grow side by side. It is beyond human power to separate them. We have to let them grow together and in time they will separate themselves. That's the gospel truth.

In the Church the more enthusiasm we have, the more likely we are to run up against small minds, rigid minds, narrow minds and stony hearts. Even if we are lovers of order we are just as likely to be frustrated by the spirit blowing where the spirit will.

Our churches and our lives will always be untidy, riddled with contradictions. There will always be a sinful side and a virtuous side, a dark side and a bright side, a despairing side and one full of hope.

We shouldn't be surprised if the people of God are imperfect, simply because people are imperfect.

# A Life Perspective

If God were to grant you seventy years of life, you would spend:

24 years sleeping
14 years working
8 years in amusement
6 years at the dinner table
5 years travelling
4 years in conversation
3 years in education
3 years reading
3 years watching television

If you went to church every Sunday and prayed for five minutes every morning and night, you would be giving God five months of your life.

Can't we give five months out of seventy years?

# Tradition

Change is difficult to effect. I remember hearing a story about a church that had a row of seats on which nobody ever sat. It had become a tradition that there was something special about this row. If visitors sat there by accident ushers would ask them to leave the seats because this was a sacred space.

Legends grew as to why this was such a sacred place. One tradition held it was reserved for the presence of Jesus. Others said it was something more sinister – that people had sat there and some evil had befallen them because they did. There were as many legends as there were people.

Recently the village and the congregation grew when a new housing estate was built. So the minister decided to get to the bottom of the mystery. After days going through the parish records he found an entry written by one of his predecessors over eighty years earlier. It said: 'The parish doesn't have enough money to fix the leak in the roof so we covered the fifth pew with a sheet to protect it. A bucket was placed on the pew to catch the water.' Years after the roof was repaired, people still avoided the fifth pew and found a 'holy' reason to justify a tradition.

Custom and tradition are mixed blessings. They can be wise guides to the future, or they can handcuff us to the past. No wonder Jesus condemned those 'who worship only with their lips while their hearts are far from me'.

# Turning to God

There are times in life when everything is hopeless and yet when we've lived through them there is a sense that, having fought the good fight, there's nothing left to do but experience God's help. In our brokenness, we allow God to help us more than in times of strength. I know many people who have prayed whole-heartedly for a cure but who eventually succumb to death. There was a satisfaction that having prayed as diligently as we did, there was nothing else we could do. We did our best. We didn't get the result we wanted, but because we did all we could, there must be a reason for it.

# A Little Glimpse of Eternity

I was walking earlier this morning in the beautiful Fermanagh countryside. The leaves crunched under my feet, the air was crisp and the sky was pale blue. I puffed and panted as I pushed my ageing body up the hillside. I turned around to take in the magnificent autumn view when I reached the top. That was when I thanked God for 'this little glimpse of eternity' in my own backyard.

# Looking For the Best in Everyone

Jesus makes a point in the gospels and it is this: 'Anyone who is not against us, is for us.' That's an amazing quote. It's exactly the opposite of what the Church thinks and what we usually would think about ourselves. Churches the world over have fought wars thinking that those who are not for them must be against them. And we are the same. That's the small-mindedness that is rejected by Jesus. He turns it around and looks at it positively and says, 'Anyone who is not against you is for you.' There's a world of difference in that.

For example, many parents wonder about their children not going to Mass. The whole point is this. It would be lovely if everybody went to Mass and it's a central part of Christian community. But just because people don't go to God the same way as us doesn't mean they are against us. In fact, Jesus says if they are not against you, if they are not actively against you, then you can take it for granted they are for you. That's the distinction between a miserly religion and an open one such as Jesus wants us to have.

We are to see good – not bad – in others. And the same with ourselves. Sometimes we see the worst enemy that is within ourselves.

Try looking for what is best.

# Home is Where We
# Start From

I was reading a poem by T. S. Eliot recently and a phrase jumped out at me: 'Home is where we start from.'

It set me thinking about the journeys of life. I've got to that age. The earlier part of life can be consumed with untamed rushing at life. My own was filled with impatience to get things done, a longing to achieve something. But I discovered at some point that life had passed me by. I realised I was so far down the road of life that the journey home stared me in the face. That was a mid-life crisis. I got some peace when I settled myself and recognised that I would love to be young again, but I wouldn't want all the turbulence of youth a second time. But the second half of life, I've discovered, demands a journey too. I still need many of the things I've always needed – a sense of identity, a meaning, a purpose in life, a sense of self-worth. I also need a sense of intimacy and rootedness. Perfection, like peace, comes dropping slow. Physically, spiritually and emotionally I'm reasonably content with where I am at and don't need to be 'on the road' all the time.

That's why the words of T. S. Eliot meant so much to me. 'Home is where we start from.'

# Letting Go

I was reading from the Book of Job in Morning Prayer recently and I was struck by something that I've read for over forty years without noticing its importance. It said, 'Naked I came from my mother's womb and naked I'll go back.'

That gave me a clue. Peace in the second half of life is about letting go. Mostly we let go of all the things we tried so hard to attain in the first half of life.

But as I think about it now, the things we need to let go most of all are our hurts, fears and wounds. I find most peace when I learn to forgive – others, God and myself. It's impossible to go through life without being wounded. We can't have everything we dreamed of. There's disappointment and anger within us and unless I learn to forgive, I'll give way to bitterness.

# A Short Guide to a Successful Life

See everything.
Overlook a great deal.
Improve a little.

*– Pope John XXIII*

# Don't Let the Sun Go Down on Your Anger

Always set up a time and a place for confrontation. It is important not to blow off steam without thinking. But it is equally important to make a time and place to talk. Don't let it seethe beneath the surface. Face up to it.

The time and place should be reasonably suitable for both parties. Big problems early in the morning are not advisable. A suitable time is important. Find a quiet place where you'll be undisturbed.

No TV. No distractions. No in-laws. No children.

### Know What the Fight is About

Many angry people don't know what they are angry about. The issue they think is important isn't the real one, but it's the only one that is manageable right now.

The real issue is suppressed and a little too sensitive to bring to the surface.

Ask yourself: What's really bugging me in this situation? Am I over-reacting? Is it worth all the hassle? If you can put your finger on the trouble state it clearly. Don't conceal it in a mist of words and feelings.

### State Your Case – Don't Accuse

In stating your case use 'I-statements'. Don't accuse the other person. If you don't make 'I-statements' you end up being accusatory: 'You're always worrying,' 'You never talk to me.'

I-statements' make us deal with facts. They are the difference between venting your anger on the other person and reporting your true feelings. Telling busy people that they never talk to you is not helpful. Saying that perhaps they should work less and make time for you is more helpful.

### Listen

This is a lot more difficult than it seems. It means sitting on the edge of your seat trying to discover what the other person is really saying, even more than concentrating on what to say next, or on being right.

To make sure you've got it right, you should now and then summarise what you think the other person is saying.

Body language is the best clue to whether you're listening or not. Eyes that fidget, a glazed look, writing, reading, sneaking a look at the TV will all give the game away.

# The Quality of Mercy

Everyone has known people who kept every law and every commandment, but were spiteful, bitter, small-minded, bigoted bullies.

There is no holiness where such attitudes thrive. The spiritual life will be blessed with a good spirit, the 'other' life deals with the bad spirits. I don't want to call it evil, but at the moment I can think of no other word for the destruction these 'holy' tyrants cause. There is nothing so detrimental to genuine holiness as a person who keeps all the rules but whose 'god' spreads unhappiness.

I am always reminded of the elder son in the story of the prodigal son. You couldn't fault him for duty, but he wasn't able to celebrate and made himself a sad rejected figure. Holy people should be merciful to themselves and others. They spread peace, understanding and compassion.

# The Dangers of Slander

The slanderous tongue kills three: the slandered, the slanderer and he who listens to slander.

*– The Talmud*

# Accepting Difference

Anyone on a spiritual journey needs to have the ability to accept difference. I don't have to be perfect myself and I shouldn't expect others to be perfect. I need to seek and be friends with those who are different. Jesus said that we should leave the 99 to look after themselves and go after the one who is lost. I need to respect myself when I am lost and I have to help others when they are lost. Those who are lost are also on a journey.

Grace builds on nature so I need to make sure I am healthy and happy within myself. I have to tackle whatever is humanly dysfunctional.

If I do that, God's grace will do the rest.

# Just Do It

Whatever we learn to do, we learn by actually doing it. Men come to be builders, for instance, by building, and harp players by playing the harp. In the same way, by doing just acts we come to be just; by doing self-controlled acts we come to be self-controlled; and by doing brave acts we become brave.

*– Aristotle*

# A Principled Journey

I want to share a few rules that I use in determining my own spiritual journey. Because I am a Christian, they will focus on Christian spirituality. To me there are a number of essential principles I have to get right in my life if I'm to be honest before God.

First, I have to have personal integrity. I must be able to look at myself in the mirror and be honest. I have to know that I'm not a sham.

Second, if I am to be serious about having a Christian spiritual journey, it is absolutely essential that I do everything I can to help the poor. The poor at home, the poor in the Developing World, the spiritually poor as well as the materially poor.

Third, I must have community somewhere in my life. There can be no communion unless I have community. And if there is no communion there's no Eucharist, and if there is no Eucharist there is no Christianity.

Fourth, it is most important that a person who is genuinely trying to be holy should have a peacefulness and quietness about them. They should be easy to live with.

# The Special Child

The child, yet unborn, spoke with the Father,
'Lord, how will I survive in the world?
I will not be like other children. My
walk may be slower, my speech hard
to understand. I may look different.
What is to become of me?'
The Lord replied to the child,
'My precious one, have no fear, I will
give you exceptional parents; they
will love you because you are special,
not in spite of it. Though your path
through life will be difficult, your
reward will be greater, you will have been blessed
with a special ability to love,
and those whose lives you touch will be blessed
because you are special.'

# The Wisdom of Aesop

From Aesop's fables comes this little reminder about vanity and self-discipline.

A coal-black crow once stole a piece of meat. She flew to the tree and held the meat in her beak.

A fox who saw her wanted the meat for himself, so he looked up the tree and said, 'How beautiful you are, my friend. Your feathers are fairer than the dove's. Is your voice as sweet as your form is beautiful? If so you must be the queen of the birds.'

The crow was so happy in his praise that she opened her mouth to show how she could sing. Down fell the piece of meat.

The fox seized upon it and ran away.

Aesop also supplies a simple little story about compassion. One day a great lion lay asleep in the sunshine. A little mouse ran across his paw and wakened him. The great lion was going to eat him up when the little mouse cried, 'Oh please, let me go, sir. Some day I may help you.'

The lion laughed at the idea that the little mouse could be of any help to him. But he was a good-natured lion and he set the mouse free.

Not long afterwards, the lion got caught in a net. He tugged and pulled with all his might, but the net was too strong. Then he roared loudly. The little mouse heard him and ran to the spot.

'Be still, dear lion, and I will set you free. I will gnaw the ropes.'

With his sharp little teeth the mouse cut through the net, and the lion came out of the net.

'You laughed at me once,' said the mouse. 'You thought I was too little to do you a good turn. But you see that you owe your life to a little mouse.'

Which shows that compassion lies within the power of the mighty and the meek.

<<<<<<<<<<<<<<<<<<<<<<<<<<<<<<<<<<<<<<<<<<<<<<<<<<<<<

# A Short Course in Human Relations

The six most important words:
'I admit I made a mistake.'
The five most important words:
'You did a good job.'
The four most important words:
'What is your opinion?'
The three most important words:
'If you please.'
The two most important words:
'Thank you.'
The one most important word:
'We.'
The least important word:
'I.'

# Keep an Open Mind

Closed-minded people put others down;
Open-minded people are tolerant and
  understanding.
Closed-minded people cannot see the good
  in people who disagree with them;
Open-minded people see some good in
  everyone.
Closed-minded people mind other people's
  business;
Open-minded people mind their own.
Closed-minded people are envious and
  jealous;
Open-minded people are contented and
  thankful.
Closed-minded people know it all;
Open-minded people realise how little we
  all know.
Closed-minded people belittle our cultures
  and customs;
Open-minded people know the value of
  diversity.
Closed-minded people are suspicious and
  overly cautious;
Open-minded people are trusting and
  adventurous.
Closed-minded people talk without thinking;

Open-minded people think before talking.
Closed-minded people think they are
     always right;
Open-minded people realise how easy it is
     to be wrong.
Closed-minded people like to judge others;
Open-minded people let others judge them.
Closed-minded people form opinions
     without information;
Open-minded people value facts before
     opinion.
Closed-minded people are self-centred;
Open-minded people put others before
     themselves.
Which are you – open-minded or closed-
     minded?

# Part 2

# Having a Laugh

# Too Much of a Good Thing

A young preacher was asked to give a sermon in a small country church. He was disappointed to find that there was only one man, an elderly farmer, in the congregation.

Asked if he wished to hear the sermon, the farmer said, 'Well if I took a bucket of meal down to the yard and only one chicken turned up, I'd feed her.'

So the preacher delivered his sermon, which took about an hour and a half. Afterwards he asked the old man what he thought of it. 'Well,' was the reply, 'if I took a bucket full of meal down to the yard and only one chicken turned up, I'd feed her, of course, but I'm blowed if I'd give her the whole bucketful!'

# Things We Would Like To Believe

That a church really did put up a notice:
'Pray now and avoid the Christmas rush.'

That some schoolboys really did write in their essays that Salome danced in front of Harrods.

# Paradise

An Englishman, a Frenchman and a Russian were studying a picture of Adam and Eve in the Garden of Eden. 'They are obviously English,' said the Englishman, 'she's only got one apple but she is giving it to him to eat.' 'No, no,' said the Frenchman, 'if they are naked and eating fruit together, they must be French.' 'They are Russian,' said the Russian firmly. 'They have no clothes, hardly anything to eat, and yet they think they are in paradise.'

# Family Ties

There was a car accident in a small town. A crowd surrounded the victim, so the newspaper reporter couldn't manage to get close enough to see.

He hit upon a bright idea. 'I'm the father of the victim,' he cried, 'please let me through!'

The crowd let him pass so that he was able to get right up to the scene of he accident where he discovered, to his embarrassment, that the victim was a donkey.

# Senior Citizens

If you are not sure that you qualify as a true senior citizen, the following checklist may be of help: Everything hurts – and what doesn't hurt doesn't work.

- The gleam in your eye is the sun shining on your bifocals.
- You feel like the morning after ... but you haven't been anywhere.
- You get winded playing cards and your little black book contains only the names of medical specialists.
- Your children begin to look middle-aged.
- A dripping tap causes an uncontrollable urge.
- You join a health club – and don't go.
- You have all the answers, but no one asks the questions.
- You look forward to a dull evening.
- You need glasses to find your glasses.
- You turn the lights down for economy instead of romance.
- You sit in a rocking chair but can't make it go.
- Your knees buckle, but your belt won't.
- Your back goes out more often than you do.
- You put your bra on back to front and it fits better.
- Your house is too big and your medicine cabinet too small.

- You sink your teeth into a steak and they stay there.

- Your birthday cake collapses under the weight of the candles.

- You decide to live long enough to be a problem to your kids and get your own back.

<><><><><><><><><><><><><><><><><><><><><><><><><><><><><><><><><><><><><><>

# Going Nuts

Somebody sent me one of those inspirational cards recently. It said, *God wants spiritual fruits; not religious nuts.* That's good advice. We can waste a lot of energy doing so-called 'religious' things. God would much prefer us to help our neighbour in a practical way.

Speaking of nuts, reminds me of the man who visited his elderly relative in the nursing home. She was sleeping gently so he waited beside her bed. There was a bowl of nuts on her table. He took one and before long he'd finished the lot. He had to own up when she awoke. 'I'm sorry auntie, I've eaten all your nuts,' he said apologetically. 'Oh don't worry, James,' she said. 'Once I've sucked the chocolate off them, I don't eat the nuts anyway.'

# Old Puns Never Die

Old foresters never die,
they only lose their bark.
Old thieves never die,
they only steal away.
Old gardeners never die,
they only go to seed.
Old snooker players never die,
they only go to pot.
Old prime ministers never die,
they just hide in the cabinet.
Old bakers never die,
they knead the dough too much.
Old vampires never die,
they just grow long in the tooth.
Old dancers never die,
they just go-go on for ever.
Old insurance men never die,
it's against their policies.
Old cleaners never die,
they just kick the bucket.
Old bank managers never die,
they just lose interest.

# A Good Sales Pitch

The young salesman had failed to make his sale. He thought to himself: 'It just proves you can lead a horse to water, but can't make him drink.' 'Son,' said the sales manager, 'let me give you a piece of advice. Your job is not to make him drink, it's to make him thirsty.'

# Avoidance Tactics

Ten ways to avoid life's tribulations:
1. Take a pen to the bank.
2. Take toilet paper to the pub.
3. Never book a flight on bank holidays.
4. Get a gas barbecue.
5. Wear earplugs in the dentist's waiting room.
6. Take your own radio when staying in hotels.
7. Give up supporting whatever team frustrates.
8. Rent a DVD if you are planning to watch TV on a Saturday night.
9. Have a decent meal before going out to eat at a nouvelle cuisine restaurant.
10. Concrete the garden.

# Confusion

If you think you are confused, consider poor Columbus. He didn't know where he was going, and when he got there, he didn't know where he was, and when he got back, he didn't know where he had been.

# Toot and Tell

There was a priest who was transferred to a parish near Las Vegas. He was full of brilliant ideas and began to learn how to sell his products by looking at how they did it on the Strip. He was very successful and the crowds began to come. This aroused the interest of the bishop who came to visit him. He stayed a few days and he was impressed by some of the things his priest did. He called him aside and he explained to him that the drive-through confessional he had started was a terrific idea. He was also very impressed by this new 24-hour service he was offering as it helped a lot of people who did shifts to be able to come. 'But,' said the bishop, 'I have to draw a line at this flashing neon sign which says "TOOT AND TELL OR GO TO HELL". That simply is taking things too far and it has got to go.'

# The Three Gifts

There was a mother who had three very successful sons. They decided to make her birthday very special for her. The first one was a builder so he bought a huge mansion for his mother. There were nine bedrooms in it, twelve bathrooms, garages and God knows what else. The second son thought he would buy her a top-of-the -range Mercedes. The third son knew his mother was religious so he decided to get her something special. He travelled the world and eventually found a rare and wonderful parrot that could repeat random verses from the Bible.

A month later they visited her and each wanted to know how his gift had been received. The mother said to the first one, 'Well, the house was beautiful, but I have discovered I can only sleep in one room at a time. And all these rooms have to be cleaned. My little old house could be done in half an hour. I wish I were back in my old house.' To the second son who bought the Mercedes, she said, 'It is a beautiful car and it is very comfortable. But I'm afraid I'll scratch it. I was far more comfortable in my old banger.' To the third son she said, 'I have to say it was a wonderful present, because that little bird you bought me was the tastiest bit of chicken I have ever eaten in my life.'

# How Do Wars Start?

A nine-year-old asked his father, 'Dad, how do wars start?'

'Well, son,' his father began, 'take World War I. That war started when Germany invaded Belgium ...'

'Just a minute,' his wife interrupted. 'It began when Archduke Franz Ferdinand of Austria was assassinated by a Serbian nationalist.'

'Well, dear, that was the spark that ignited the fighting, but the political and economic factors leading to the war had been in place for some time.'

'Yes, I know, honey, but our son asked how the war began and every history book says that World War I began with the murder of Archduke Franz Ferdinand of Austria.'

Drawing himself up with an air of superiority, the husband snapped, 'Are you answering the question, or am I?'

The wife turned her back on him in a huff, stalked out of the room and slammed the door behind her.

When the dishes stopped rattling, an uneasy silence followed. The nine-year-old then broke the silence: 'Dad, you don't have to say any more about how wars start. I understand now.'

# Bats in the Belfry

Three priests got together one day while they were out playing golf. They talked, like most priests do, about deep spiritual matters – the things that really matter. So the conversation most of the day concentrated on how to get bats out of the belfry.

The first priest confessed, 'I have to admit, that even though you are not allowed to destroy bats, I got a gun, through sheer frustration, and fired it at them. All I succeeded in doing was scattering them and making three holes in the ceiling. The bats came back to their home and brought some of their friends as well.'

The second man said he did something that was much more environmentally friendly. He captured the bats in a basket and drove fifty miles away from the church and released them outside an old barn. Unfortunately, when he got home the bats had arrived back before him.

The third man said he had found the solution to the problem. 'I have no more problems with bats,' he said. 'The first thing I did was baptise them, then I confirmed them. And when I had them baptised and confirmed I never saw them in church from that day to this.'

# How to Get to Heaven

I'm sure most of you will remember when bishops used to ask the young people going for Confirmation some very hard questions. One day the bishop was examining a class and he asked them, 'What must we do to get to heaven?' Nobody said anything, so he began to prompt them.

'Supposing a person sold their house and car and gave all their money to charity, would that get them to heaven?' The class answered no.

'Supposing someone left their job and went to work in the foreign missions for nothing for ten years. Would that get them to heaven?'

Again the class answered no.

He had another go at it: 'Supposing someone was very good to their children, husband, wife, neighbours and even animals, would that get them to heaven?'

Again the children answered no.

The bishop was getting a little frustrated at this time so he asked them, 'Well, what must you do to get to heaven?' One wee fellow shot up his hand and said, 'To get to heaven you've got to die first.'

# Getting into
# Heaven

I was down at a wedding in Clare. One of the pair getting married was a solicitor. And, as you know, I have great time for lawyers but very little time for law. So I thought of a little story about a couple who were going out together and sadly were killed and went to heaven. Peter let them into heaven, which means you can get into heaven even though you are *not* married. When they got to heaven they kept pestering Peter to get married. Peter said, 'You don't need to get married. This is heaven. You are supposed to be happy here.'

But they kept pestering him. After about a century he called them aside one day and said, 'OK. I have the priest ready. You can get married now.' Which they did. And the marriage lasted about thirty years and then they started looking for a divorce. So they went to Peter and said, 'Could we get a divorce?' Peter said, 'Well, it has taken me a hundred years to get a priest into heaven to marry you. How long do you think it's going to take me to get a lawyer into heaven to get you a divorce?'

# My Husband is a Saint

Two old Dublin ladies were talking about saints. One of them leaned across the fence and said, 'Mary, you know my husband is a pure saint.' To which Mary replied, 'Well, Bridget you are lucky, because mine is still alive.'

I suppose that's what makes a saint anyway. You have to be dead first.

# Religion Class

One day in religion class the subject was the Ten Commandments, and the class had reached the last one. When the teacher asked if anyone could state what the tenth commandment was, young Donald waved his hand wildly.

When asked he stood up proudly and gave his answer: 'Thou shalt not take the covers off thy neighbour's wife.'

Later, during a lesson on the story of the Prodigal Son, the teacher asked: 'In the midst of all the celebration for the prodigal son, there was one for whom the feast brought no joy, only bitterness. Can you tell me who it was?

Donald was once again pleased to be asked and replied: 'The fatted calf.'

# Two Loose Ladies

A woman came to a priest one day to say that she had bought two parrots. They were two lady parrots. They were recommended as being top-class talking parrots. But when she got them home and put them in a cage all the two parrots would say is, 'We're two loose ladies, do you want a good time?' After a week this began to annoy her intensely, so she sought the advice of the priest. What should she do? Would he come down and bless them?

The priest thought of the two parrots he himself had bought. They were two male parrots, called Moses and Jacob, and he had trained them well. They could pray, they could quote the Bible, they could even sing a hymn, given the right birdseed. His suggestion was simple. His parrots couldn't go to her house in case they would be brought down to the level of the two ladies, so the two ladies would have to come to his house. In no time at all they would join the men in praying, reading the Bible and singing hymns.

The woman brought her two parrots to the house and when she entered Moses and Jacob were in their cages saying the Rosary.

The two ladiy parrots were put in a cage and, right enough, they were as friendly as ever. The first thing they said was, 'Hi, we're two loose ladies, do you want a good time?' At that Jacob looked over at Moses and said, 'Moses, you can drop the rosary beads, our prayers have been answered.'

# Spousal Support

I want to share a letter a colleague sent me. It was probably doing the rounds on the internet. One piece of advice – *please* read right to the end!

Dear Friends,

It is important for men to remember that, as women grow older, it becomes harder for them to maintain the same quality of housekeeping as when they were younger. When you notice this, try not to yell at them. Some are oversensitive, and there's nothing worse than an oversensitive woman.

My name is Jim. Let me relate how I handled the situation with my wife, Peggy. When I retired a few years ago, it became necessary for Peggy to get a full-time job along with her part-time job for extra income. Shortly after she started working, I noticed she was beginning to show her age. I usually get home from the golf club about the same time she gets home from work. Although she knows how hungry I am, she almost always says she has to rest for half an hour or so before she starts dinner. I don't yell at her. Instead, I tell her to take her time and just wake me when she gets dinner on the table. When doing simple jobs, she seems to think she needs more rest periods. She had to take a break when she was only half finished mowing the lawn. I try not to make a scene. I'm a fair man. I tell her to get herself a nice, big, cold glass of freshly squeezed orange juice, and just sit for a while. And, as long as she is making one for herself, she may as well make one for me too. I know that I probably look like a saint in the way I support Peggy. I'm not saying that showing this much consideration is easy. Many men will find it difficult. Some will find it impossible! Nobody knows better than I do how frustrating women get as they get older. However, guys, even if you just use a little more tact and less criticism of your ageing wife because of this article, I will consider that writing it was well worth while. After all, we are put on this earth to help each other.

Yours helpfully,
Jim

*Editor's Note:*
Jim died suddenly on 27 May of a perforated intestine. The police report says he was found with a Callaway extra long 50-inch Big Bertha Driver 11 golf club jammed up his rear end, with barely five inches of grip showing and a sledgehammer lying nearby. His wife Peggy was arrested and charged with murder. The all-woman jury took only fifteen minutes to find her not guilty, accepting her defence that Jim had accidentally sat on his golf club.

# Status Symbol

A man wanted to get himself a new high-performance car which would also be a status symbol. So he went to the local Redemptorist monastery and said, 'I want to buy a Lexus, would you say a novena for me?' The priest asked him, 'What's a Lexus?'

'It's a high-performance car, a status symbol, and I want to get one and would you please say a novena that I will get one?' The priest replied, 'Oh we wouldn't say a novena for anything like that, but maybe if you go up to Ardoyne to the Passionists, they might.' So off he went to the Passionists and presented his request. The Passionists said, 'We wouldn't say a novena for a thing like that, but if you go to Brian D'Arcy in The Graan he'll do anything.' So off he went to The Graan and he met Fr Brian there and said, 'Fr Brian, would you say a novena for me? I want to get a Lexus.'

Fr Brian said, 'What's a novena?'

# Bargaining Power

A little boy had seen a lovely red bike in the local store and he demanded that his mother get it. The mother decided that he had to earn it. 'I'll make a bargain with you,' she said. 'If you can keep your room tidy, then we can discuss this again next Monday.' So the boy worked very hard at keeping his room clean. Several plastic bags were filled with rubbish and eventually a floor was discovered.

Monday arrived and he thought he was sure to get his red bike. The mother pointed out that that was only the start. He was doing very badly at school. 'If you study enough this week, then we'll talk about it next Monday.'

The young boy wasn't going to school for nothing. He knew this was a tactic that wasn't going to work so he thought he'd adopt more direct approach. He sat down at his computer to write a letter to God. He began, 'Dear God, I'm the best boy in the world.'

Even he knew that he wasn't the best boy in the world and since God knows all things God was likely to know that too. So he deleted and started again, 'Dear God, I'm as good a boy as you made me ... ' But he knew that mightn't work either.

Then he noticed a lovely statue of Our Lady in his mother's room.

He went back to his computer and began to write, 'Dear God, if you ever want to see your mother again ...'

# Definitions

*Amen:* The only part of a prayer that everyone knows.

*Bulletin:* Your receipt for attending church.

*Choir:* A group of people whose singing allows the rest of us to lipsync.

*Holy water:* A liquid whose chemical formula is $H_2OLY$.

*Hymn:* A song of praise, usually sung in a key three octaves higher than the congregation's range.

*Recessional hymn:* The last song of the service, often sung quietly since most of the people have already left.

*Incense:* Holy Smoke!

*Jonah:* The original 'Jaws' story.

*Justice:* When kids have kids of their own.

*Pew:* A medieval torture device still found in Catholic churches.

*Procession:* The ceremonial formation at the beginning of the service consisting of servers, the readers, the celebrant, and late worshippers looking for seats.

*Recessional:* The ceremonial procession at the conclusion of the service led by the congregation trying to beat the crowd to the car park.

*Ten Commandments:* The most important Top Ten list not given by David Letterman.

*Ushers:* The only people in the church who don't know the seating capacity of a pew.

# Hearing Test

There is a lovely wee story about a husband who was worried that his wife was going deaf. This man went to the doctor because any suggestion that his wife might be getting old would not have been well received. He asked the doctor for help.

The doctor suggested a little experiment. 'Stand about fifteen feet away from your wife and ask her a question. If she answers it she is okay. If she doesn't, go a little bit closer and ask the same question. If she answers it she is probably okay but if she doesn't she might have some mild deafness. Finally, go about three feet away from her and ask the same question. By that stage you will know how deaf she is.

At home his wife was cooking the evening meal. He stood at the dining room door: 'What have we got for tea this evening, darling?' There was no answer. So he went to the kitchen door: 'What have we got for tea this evening, darling?' No answer. Then he went right up to her, beside the cooker: 'What have we got for tea this evening, darling?' She gave him a look that would turn milk and snapped: 'I've told you three times already. It's roast chicken.'

# A Blast from the Past

Did you hear about the old lady who was in court for the first time at the grand old age of eighty-three? The prosecuting counsel tried his best to make her feel at home in the strange surroundings of the courtroom. 'Mrs Smith, you know me, don't you?' he began.

'Of course I know you, you're Donald Jones. I have known you since you were in nappies. You think you're the most important barrister in the country, but behind it all you are the same young delinquent teenager who broke into our orchard and stole our best apples every September. Your poor mother never had a moment's peace with you.'

'Now, now, Mrs Smith,' Mr Jones said, trying to talk above the laughter echoing around the room, 'Try to keep you answers brief and to the point. Do you know that man over there?' He pointed to the defence barrister.

'Yes I do,' Mrs Jones replied disdainfully. 'That's William Murphy whom everybody knows to be a cheat and a gambler and he drinks too much as well.'

Mr Murphy buried his face in his hands. The judge lifted his gavel and pounded the bench to restore order. He called the prosecuting barrister to the bench. 'Mark my words,' he said in an audible whisper. 'If you ask her whether she knows me, I'll have you thrown in jail for contempt immediately.'

# The Pope at the Wailing Wall

The Pope was being watched by a little man from Belfast. He wasn't sure what the Pope was doing, so he asked an American cardinal. And the American cardinal told him that he was praying for America, for the American people, for the safety of their troops across the world, for victory over Al Qaida, and for those who died in the 9/11 attack.

The wee man was impressed. But he then went further along the wall and he asked a man who turned out to be a rabbi what the Pope was praying for. And he told him the Pope was praying for Jews and for peace between Jews and Arabs and between Israel and Lebanon and for the chosen people. Then he noticed that there was an Irish bishop standing beside him and he asked him what the Pope was doing at the Wailing Wall. And the Irish bishop said, 'Well, of course the Pope spends his days praying for Ireland.' He was praying for peace between Protestants and Catholics, between Unionists and Nationalists. And most of all he was praying that the Paisleyites and the Sinn Féiners would get together and work for peace. And the wee man turned away and said, 'No wonder the poor man's talking to the wall.'

# Coming Unstuck

There's a lovely story about a Dublin man who took on a job driving a lorry. He had a big load to deliver down to Kerry one day. Whilst he was going through Killarney he saw a sign that read 'Low Bridge Detour'. But the Dub thought he could get through anywhere in Kerry. He got to the low bridge and was going through nice and slowly and the next thing, crunch! There he was stuck in the middle of the bridge. He couldn't go backwards or forwards and didn't know what to do. Most of us would panic, but not the Dub.

He took out a packet of cigarettes and lit one and was smoking away, wondering what he should do, when and a Kerry Garda came up and knocked the window. 'Are we stuck?' said the Garda. 'Ah no, I'm just having a wee smoke,' said the Dub. 'Well what are we doing out in the middle of the road then?' says the Garda. 'What have you got in your lorry?' 'Ah, don't worry! I'm delivering bridges,' says the Dub.

# Mixed Blessings

I heard a nice little story about a man from East Belfast who came from a puritan background and wasn't allowed to back horses, but he had this urge to do so. So he went down to the Curragh in Kildare, thinking he'd be unknown down there. In the first two races he nearly lost his shirt. He had kept a few euros to get him home and he went out the back of the stand to calm himself down.

There he saw the horses parading for third race and he noticed that there was a priest who went in, looked at them all and then went over gently to one of them and made what looked like the sign of the cross on the horse's forehead. He looked at the number of the horse but saw that it was a 50–1 chance, so he wouldn't back it. He had lost enough already. But lo and behold, didn't the horse win by about five lengths.

For the next race he watched what the priest did and this time it was a 30–1 horse he crossed, so he put a few euro on it and luckily it won. The same happened in the fifth and sixth races. By now he had accumulated a couple of hundred euro. Before the last race he went to the ring to observe the priest again. Not only did he mark the horse's forehead but he put a cross on his ears, his eyes, his nostrils and even on his hooves. He put on every cent he had in his pockets. The horse ran about a hundred yards and then, puffed out, it walked back to the start again. He had lost everything. Very annoyed, he went to the priest and asked him why he had let him down. And the priest said to him, 'That's the difficulty with you people from East Belfast. You don't know the difference between a blessing and the last rites.'

# Seeing Eye to Eye

One day a priest who was pastor of a New York church discovered that, for no apparent reason, an elderly lady in his parish had taken a vehement dislike to him and made no secret of the fact. She told everyone she met she couldn't abide him. And, as is the case in all small parishes, word eventually reached the pastor himself

He dreaded the day when parish calls would take him to her door. And, when the day came, he paced back and forth in front of the building, trying to work up the courage to go in.

He was secretly hoping she would not be home and he was praying he would be able to leave his card and exit discreetly. So he climbed the stairs and knocked on the door. There was no answer.

He knocked again and heard a sound inside, so he knelt down and looked through the letterbox to see if anyone was there. To his surprise he saw an eye staring back at him.

With a chuckle the woman remarked, 'Father, this is the first time we have seen eye to eye!'

'Yes,' he replied, 'and we had to get down on our knees to do it!'

# Rudolph

A Russian couple were walking down the street in Moscow one night when the man felt a drop hit his nose.

'I think it's raining,' he said to his wife.

'No, that felt more like snow to me,' she replied.

'I'm sure it was just rain,' he said.

Just then they saw a Communist Party official walking towards them.

'Let's not fight about it,' the man said. 'Let's ask Comrade Rudolph whether it's officially raining or snowing.'

As the official approached, the man said, 'Tell us, Comrade Rudolph, is it officially raining or snowing?'

'It's raining, of course,' he replied, and walked on.

But the woman insisted: 'I know that felt like snow!'

The man quietly replied: 'Rudolph the Red knows rain, dear.'

# The Value of Old Age

We old folk are very valuable:
We have gold in our teeth
Silver in our kidneys
Gas in our stomachs
And lead in our feet.

# A Good Example

There is a story told about a man who meets a beggar in the street one day. He's a shabby-looking homeless man and he asks him for money to buy a meal. The man is feeling good that day so he takes €10 out of his wallet and begins to ask him questions. He says, 'I want to make sure you are not going to spend this money on drink.' The beggar tells him, 'Drink is what put me on the street. I gave it up years ago. I'm never likely to go back on it again.' 'Maybe with that rattly cough you have it's smoking that you spend your money on.' The beggar replied, 'I never smoked in my life. And the rattly cough is from sleeping out in the damp streets for ten years.'

'I hope you wouldn't go and spend it on a horse?' To which the beggar replies, 'Gambling is a mug's game. I don't have a penny to gather enough food, so I'm not likely to waste it on a horse I don't even know.'

'Well, there's a red-light district just around the corner. How do I know you're not going to spend the money there?' The beggar answered, 'Can you not see that a homeless, dirty, smelly old beggar like me wouldn't get anywhere even in a red-light district for €100, never mind €10?'

The man finally gave in and said, 'Well I'm not going to give you the €10. Instead I'm going to bring you home and I'm going to ask my wife to cook you the best meal you have ever had.'

The homeless man was amazed. 'Won't your wife be furious with you for doing that? I'm dirty and smelly and she won't want me in your house.'

To which the man replied, 'Don't worry about that. I just want my wife to see what happens a man who doesn't drink, smoke, gamble or go with women.'

# Methuselah's Menu

Methuselah ate what he found on his plate,
And never, as people do now,
Did he note the amount of the calorie
    count;
He ate it because it was chow.
He wasn't disturbed as at dinner he sat,
Devouring a roast or a pie,
To think it was lacking the right kind of fat
Or a couple of vitamins shy.
He cheerfully chewed each species of food,
Unmindful of troubles or fears
Lest his health might be hurt
By some fancy dessert;
And he lived over 900 years!

# My Twelve Days of Christmas

On the first day of Christmas
My true love said to me:
'I'm glad we bought fresh turkey
And a proper Christmas tree.'
On the second day of Christmas
Much laughter could be heard
As we tucked into our turkey,
A most delicious bird.
On the third day we entertained
The people from next door.
The turkey tasted just as good
As it had the day before.
Day four, relations came to stay;
Poor Gran is looking old.
We finished up the Christmas pud
And ate the turkey cold.
On the fifth day of Christmas
Outside the snow flakes flurried.
But we were nice and warm inside
For we had our turkey curried.
On the sixth day I must admit
The Christmas spirit died.
The children fought and bickered;
We ate turkey rissoles fried.
On the seventh day of Christmas

My true love he did wince
When he sat at the table
And was offered turkey mince.
Day eight, the nerves were getting frayed
The dog had run for shelter
I served up turkey pancakes
With a glass of Alka Seltzer.
On the ninth day our cat left home
By lunchtime Dad was blotto.
He said he had to have a drink
To face turkey risotto.
By the tenth day the booze had gone
Except for our home-made brew.
And if that wasn't bad enough
We suffered turkey stew.
On the eleventh day of Christmas
The Christmas tree was moulting.
The mince pies were as hard as rock
And the turkey was revolting.
On the twelfth day my true love
Had a smile upon her lips:
The guests had gone, the turkey too,
And we dined on fish and chips.

# The Hereafter

The other day the minister came to call.
He said that at my time of life
I should be thinking about the hereafter.
I told him that I did that all the time,
Whether I'm in the kitchen or the dining-
    room
Or the bedroom or the garden,
I stop and think: 'What am I here after?'

# Part 3

# Prayers & Reflections

# God's Prayer

Most of us find prayer tough. Prayer is determined by our view of God and humankind. Why is it that we refuse to listen to Jesus telling us about the prodigal son and the host who invited everyone, even the most miserable beggar, to his table? We cling to the image of a God who is ready to avenge and punish. It's no wonder it's a grim and nerve-wracking experience to talk to such a God any time or in prayer. Who would ask him for anything? Who'd thank him for anything?

The apostles weren't afraid to ask Jesus to teach them to pray. He knew their weakness and he put them on the road to prayer. Here are a few tips.

### Prayer is a meeting

It's a meeting with God. It is not a magic formula. It is not an escape from the pressures or worries of life. In prayer, be yourself. We should not be sad clowns who hide behind smiling masks. As long as we have our masks on, nobody ever meets us. They meet, perhaps, a successful businessman, a capable teacher, a relaxed priest, a home-loving mother, an efficient secretary. But they never see the insecure, anxious, sad clowns we really are. It's a relief to show our true selves to someone who loves us. God does love you. It is easy to be yourself with him.

### We have to let God be himself

We think we know God and understand him. Somewhere in the attic of our mind we have a picture of him with a big beard. We keep bringing it out like a dog-eared photograph from the family album. No man or woman can fully understand the creator of all things. He is beyond our grasp. We will never fully understand him. So – throw away all your old notions about him. Let God come to you as he really is, not as you would have him. Be yourself and let God be himself.

### We can give him all our worries

'Come to me all you who labour and are over-burdened and I will give you rest.' Your worries obscure your vision of God. Take God at his word and give him your worries. Trust him. You will be amazed at how relieved you will feel. Once those barriers are gone, you are ready to talk to God. Use set prayers if you want to; talk to him if you are able. Sit in silence and say nothing, if that is what you prefer. Being in his presence is to be his.

### Listen!

God has given you two ears and one mouth that you may listen twice as much as you speak to him. A conversation is not only talking, but listening. You must be silent and listen to God speaking to you. You must let Jesus speak through you as well. Give him a chance ...

# Slow Me Down, Lord

Slow me down, Lord.
Ease the pounding of my heart by the
    quieting of my mind.
Steady my hurried pace with a vision of
    the eternal reach of time.
Give me, amid the confusion of the day,
The calmness of the everlasting hills.
Break the tensions of my nerves and
    muscles
With the soothing music of the singing
    streams that live in my memory.
Help me to know the magical, restoring
    power of sleep.
Teach me the art of taking minute
    vacations,
Of slowing down to look at a flower,
To chat with a friend, to pat a dog,
To read a few lines from a good book.
Slow me down, Lord, and inspire me
To send my roots deep into the soil of life's
    enduring values
That I may grow towards the stars of my
    greater destiny.

# Today

Look to this day,
For it is life,
The very life of life;
In its brief course lie all
The realities and truths of existence,
The joy of growth,
The splendour of action,
The glory of power.
For yesterday is but a memory
And tomorrow is only a vision,
But today well lived
Makes every yesterday a memory of
happiness
And every tomorrow a vision of hope.
Look well, therefore, to this day!

# An Irish Blessing

May there always be work for your hands to do.
May your purse always hold a coin or two.
May the sun always shine on our window pane.
May a rainbow be certain to follow each rain.
May the hand of a friend always be near you.
May God fill your heart with gladness to cheer you.

# God's Will

The will of God be done by us,
The law of God be kept by us,
Our evil will controlled by us,
Repentance timely made by us,
Each sinful crime be shunned by us,
Christ's Passion understood by us,
Much on our end be mused by us,
And death be blessed found by us,
With angels' music heard by us,
And God's high praises sung by us,
Forever and for aye.

– *Traditional Irish Prayer*

# Peace

Let nothing disturb thee;
Let nothing dismay thee,
All things pass.
God never changes,
Patience attains
All that it strives for.
He who has God
Finds he lacks nothing.
God alone suffices.

# Dear Friend

How are you? I just had to send a note to tell you how much I care about you.

I saw you yesterday as you were talking with your friends. I waited all day, hoping you would want to talk with me too. I gave you a sunset to close your day and a cool breeze to rest you – and I waited, You never came. It hurt me – but I still love you because I am your friend.

I saw you sleeping last night and longed to touch your brow, so I spilled moonlight upon your face. Again I waited, wanting to rush down so we could talk. I have so many gifts for you! You woke and rushed off to work. My tears were in the rain.

If you would only listen to me! I love you! I try to tell you in blue skies and in the quiet green grass. I whisper it in the leaves on the trees and breathe it in the colours of flowers, shout it to you in mountain streams, give the birds love songs to sing. I clothe you with warm sunshine and perfume the air with nature scents. My love for you is deeper than the ocean, bigger than the biggest need in your heart!

Ask me! Talk with me! Please don't forget me. I have so much to share with you!

I won't hassle you any further. It is your decision. I have chosen you and I will wait – because I love you.

Your friend,

Jesus

# A Prayer to Jesus, Our Saviour

Lord, hold my hand,
I so need your loving kindness;
Lord, hold my hand,
All through life, in joy or grief.
Lord, hold my hand,
When I'm sick with fear and anxious;
Lord, hold my hand,
In the wonder of relief.
Lord, hold my hand,
When it's dark and storms are raging;
Lord, hold my hand,
And help me live it through.
Lord, hold my hand,
When I'm lifted, joyful, loving;
Lord, hold my hand,
When I'm trying something new.
Lord, hold my hand,
When I fail or faint or waver;
Lord, hold my hand,
For I know your love is true.
Lord, hold my hand,
When I'm lonely, weary, ageing;
Lord, hold my hand,
When there's only me – and you.
Amen.

# Give Me ...

O, Lord, an ever
watchful heart
which no subtle speculation
may ever lure from Thee.
Give me a noble heart
that no unworthy affection shall
ever draw downwards to earth.
Give me a heart of honesty
that no insincerity shall warp.
Give me a heart of courage
that no distress shall ever crush
or quench.
Give me a heart so free
that no perverted or impetuous affection
shall ever claim it for its own.

*– St Thomas Aquinas*

# Healing Prayer

Lord, you invite all who are burdened to
    come to you,
Allow your healing hand to heal me.
Touch my soul with your compassion for
    others.
Touch my heart with your courage and
    infinite love for all.
Touch my mind with your wisdom that
    my mouth may always proclaim your
    praise.
Teach me to reach out to you in my need,
    and help me to lead others to you by
    my example.
Most loving heart of Jesus, bring me health
    in body and spirit that I may serve you
    with all my strength.
Touch gently this life which you have
    created, now and forever.
Amen.

# Prayer of the
# Hard-of-Hearing

Blessed are they who seem to know
That lip-reading is difficult and slow.
Blessed are they that shake my hand
And write notes to help me understand.
Blessed are those who know I long
To hear voices, music and song.
Blessed are they who seem to see
When I am lost in a group of two or three.
Blessed are those who take time out
To explain to me what they're talking about.
Blessed are they who are patient and kind
That give me comfort and peace of mind.
Blessed are they who have a smile
That makes my life the more worthwhile.
Blessed are they who make it known
By faith in God's promises, I'll not walk alone.
Blessed are they who understand
As I journey to that city 'not made with hands'.

# A Prayer

....................

Lord, make me a better person,
more considerate towards others,
more honest with myself,
more faithful to you.

Make me generous enough to want
sincerely to do your will, whatever it may be.

Help me to find my true vocation in life,
and grant that through it I may find
happiness myself and bring happiness to
others.

Grant, Lord, that those whom you call to
enter the priesthood or the religious life
may have the generosity to answer your call,
so that those who need your help may
always find it.

We ask this through Christ our Lord.

Amen.

# A Blessing

May you have:
Enough success to keep you eager,
Enough failure to keep you humble;
Enough joy to share with others,
Enough trials to keep you strong,
Enough hope to keep you happy,
Enough faith to banish depression,
Enough friends to give you comfort,
Enough determination to make each day
better than yesterday.

# A Celtic Blessing

Deep peace of the Running Wave to you.
Deep peace of the Flowing Air to you.
Deep peace of the Quiet Earth to you
Deep peace of the Shining Stars to you.
Deep peace of the Sun at Peace to you.

# A Prayer for the Stressed

.........................

Lord grant me the serenity
to accept the things
I cannot change
The courage to change the things I can
The wisdom to be careful of the toes
I step on today,
As they may be connected to the feet
I have to kiss tomorrow
Help me to give 100% at work:
12% on Monday
23% on Tuesday
40% on Wednesday
20% on Thursday
and 5% on Friday
And help me to remember
When I'm having a bad day
And it seems that people are trying
to wind me up:
It takes 42 muscles to frown
28 muscles to smile
And only 4 to extend my hand
and smack them in the mouth.

# Togetherness

Death is nothing at all – I have only slipped away into the next room. Whatever we were to each other, that we are still. Call me by my old familiar name, speak to me in the way which you always used. Laugh as we always laughed at the little jokes we enjoyed together. Play, smile, think of me, pray for me. Let my name be the household word that it always was. Let it be spoken without effort. Life means all that it ever meant. It is the same as it ever was; there is absolutely unbroken continuity. Why should I be out of your mind because I am out of your sight? I am but waiting for you, for an interval, somewhere very near just around the corner. All is well. Nothing is past; nothing is lost. One brief moment and all will be as it was before – only better, infinitely happier and for ever – we will all be one together with Christ.

# My Prayer For You

I said a prayer for you today
and know God must have heard.
I felt the answer in my heart
although he spoke no word.
I didn't ask for fame or wealth –
I know you wouldn't mind –
I asked him for a treasure
of a far more lasting kind.
I asked that he be near you
at the start of each new day,
To grant you health and blessings
and light to show your way
I asked for happiness for you
in all things great and small.
But it was his loving care
I prayed for most of all.

# Time to Listen

I tried to catch your attention this morning:

Remember when you came back to your seat and closed your eyes and put your head reverently down and talked; and talked and talked to me?

I wanted you to listen.

I wanted to tell you to open your eyes and look at my-broken body, all around you.

I am your fellow parishioner, whom you meet every day in the street, and you ignore me, busy about your own concerns

I am your next-door neighbour, whom you spend so much time gossiping about and criticising.

And it sickens me, all the coldness, all the squabbling and divisions and those endless running battles, that scourge me, and crown me with thorns.

And then you pierce my side, at Communion, with your empty words of love.

# Prayer for a Newly Married Couple

Lord, we two want to bring our life together
with you,
and we want always to continue it with you.
Help us never to hurt and never to grieve
each other.
Help us to share all our work, all our hopes,
all our dreams and all our joys.
Help us to have no secrets from each other,
so that we may be truly one.
Keep us always true to each other,
and grant that the years ahead may
draw us even closer to each other.
Grant that we may pray together and love
you in each other,
so that nothing may ever make us drift apart.
As we live with each other, help us to live
with you,
so that our love may grow perfect,
a love that is patient and kind,
a love that does not insist on its own way
a love that bears all things, believes all
things,
hopes all things, endures all things.
Give us a love like yours,
A love that never ends.

# Please Listen

If you love me, feed my sheep and start in
    your own home.
Please don't keep me at bay any longer.
Don't talk to me – listen.
I don't want you to go on loving my spirit
    and ignoring my body.
I don't want you to open your mouth to
    receive my body and close your eyes
    and ears to shut it out.
Stop thinking of me as some kind of
    spiritual being in the skies.
I am one of these people, and you cannot
    have me without them.
On the last day, I won't ask you how many
    times you attended church – that is not
    your holiness.
I will ask you how your own community,
    family and neighbours fared?
How they grew in love and faith?
How did they live their prayer?
How did your community spread its love
    within your house and across your
    neighbourhood?
Please open your eyes and ears and make
    time to listen.

# The Flawed Life

It's strange how I'm made – half mystic
and half nuts;
My eyes upon the stars, my feet deep in
the mud.
One moment I'm lying and the next I'd die
for the truth!
One moment I'm kind, big-hearted,
understanding, loyal;
The next, sneaky and cruel.
It's weird how a soul can be split up like
this –
Part God, part scallywag.
It's inconvenient too,
Because you're never quite sure which part is
on the job!
Once it used to get to me to be like that;
I hated myself ... I hated life.
I felt I'd been betrayed by God who's made me
such a mess.
What was life worth if one was so full of
flaws?
So strong, yet weak; philosopher and fool?
Yes, once because I could not be the perfect
thing I wanted to be, I hated life.
Now I know that flawed lives are good,
And serve a purpose in God's kindly plan.

Only those who've lived can feel a liar's
      shame;
Only cowards know the bitter blame
      cowards must face;
And only those who've failed can
      understand the fear of defeat.
So, through my weakness, I possess the
      key
To every heart that's sad, shamed and
      soiled.
Through my blunders, I've found tolerance
      and pity
In place of my lost pride.
So, God, I'm glad you made me as I am ...
Mystic and nut, philosopher and fool.
My eyes upon the stars, my feet deep in
      the mud.
For I've learned that flawed lives can serve
      you well.

# Could You Just
# Listen?

When I ask you to listen to me
and you start giving advice,
you have not done what I asked.
When I ask you to listen to me
and you begin to tell me why
I should not feel like that,
you are trampling on my feelings.
When I ask you to listen to me
and you feel you have to do something to
solve my problems,
you have failed me,
strange as that may seem.
Listen, all I ask is that you listen.
Advice is cheap.
When you do something for me
that I can and need to do for myself,
you contribute to my fear and inadequacy.
But when you accept as a simple fact
that I do feel what I feel,
no matter how irrational,
then I can stop trying to convince you
and get down to the business
of trying to understand it.
Irrational feelings make sense
when we understand what is behind them,

and when that is clear
the answers become obvious,
and I don't need advice.
If I want advice I will ask for it
So please, just listen.
If you want to talk,
wait a minute for your turn
and I will listen to you.

~~~~~~~~~~~~~~~~~~~~~~~~~~~~~~~~~~~~~~~~~~~~~~~~~~~~~~~~~~~~~~~

# My God Is No Stranger

I've never seen God, but I know how I feel,
It's people like you who make him 'so real'.
It seems that I pass him so often each day,
In the faces of people I meet on my way.
He's the stars in the heavens, a smile on some face,
A leaf on a tree or a rose in a vase.
He's winter and autumn and summer and spring,
In short, God is every real, wonderful thing.
I wish I might meet him much more than I do –
I would if there were more people like you.

# The Indispensable Man

Sometimes when you're feeling important
Sometimes when your ego's in bloom
Sometimes when you feel that you
Are the best qualified man in the room

Sometimes when you feel that your going
Would leave an unfillable hole
Just follow this simple instruction
And see how it humbles your soul!

Take a bucket and fill it with water,
Put your arms in it – up to the wrists
Take them out – and the hole that remains,
Is a measure of how you'll be missed!

You may splash all you please when you enter,
You may stir up the water galore,
But stop – and you'll find in a minute,
That it looks just the same as before!

The moral of this is quite simple –
Do just the best that you can,
Be proud of yourself – but remember,
There is no indispensable man!

# A Mother-in-Law's Prayer

Teach me to speak or hold my tongue:
Silence is divine.
Help me to pray to understand
This new-found child of mine.
Keep me from taking bitter sides
Or feeding angry flames,
Help me to leave them both alone
Like children at their games.
Counsel me when to call on them
And when to say goodbye,
Instruct my heart to love them both
And not ask the reason why.
Teach me to be a friend in need
Whose smile they're glad to share
Never too near, yet never too far –
This is my humble prayer.

# Prayer Before Exams

Lord, I come before you in need.
Exams are approaching,
and I am worried.
Give me courage
to face the coming weeks.
Concentrate my mind on my studies.
Help me to use my time well.
May I work hard,
but also rest and relax a little.
During each exam,
may what I study appear on the paper.
May I read each question carefully,
identify what is asked,
and answer well.
When the results come
may I be satisfied
that I did my best.
May whatever path I choose in life
bring me happiness
and give me opportunities
to better the world.
Amen.

# Myself

I have to live with myself, and so
I want to be fit for myself to know.
I want to be able as days go by,
Always to look myself straight in the eye;
I don't want to stand with the setting sun,
And hate myself for the things I've done.
I want to go out with my head erect,
I want to deserve all men's respect;
For here in the struggle for fame and self
I want to be able to like myself.
I don't want to look at myself and know
That I'm bluster and bluff and empty show:
I never can hide myself from me;
I see what others may never see.
I know what others may never know.
I never can fool myself, and so,
Whatever happens I want to be
Self-respecting and conscience free.

# Forgiveness

O Lord,
remember not only the men
and women of good will,
but also those of ill will.
But do not remember
all the suffering they
have inflicted on us;
remember the fruits
we have brought,
thanks to this suffering –
our comradeship,
our loyalty,
our humility,
our courage,
our generosity,
the greatness of
heart which has
grown out of all this –
and when they come
to judgement
let all the fruits which
we have borne
be their forgiveness.

*A prayer written by an unknown prisoner in a concentration*
*camp and left by the body of a dead child*

# Take My Hand, Lord

I cannot pray, dear Lord,
I cannot find
The hopes, recovery, health,
and peace of mind.
So, take my hand,
and take my feeble frame
And give me strength,
and help me beat my pain.

I am so weak –
give me the strength I need
To know that with your help,
we will succeed.

So help me in these long and tiring days
To know that someone sings a song of praise.
The friends who care,
who pray instead of me
For healing and a quick recovery.
So, take my hand,
and let it cling to thee
And clinging –
know no harm can come to me.

# A Dieter's Prayer

Bless my bathroom scales, O Lord,
Each week as I step on:
Help me lose a stone or two
and not put any on.

Keep me from temptation, Lord,
From chocolates and from chips:
Keep my will power going
just in case it slips.

Help me count my calories, Lord,
Steer me away from sweets:
Keep my stealthy palms away
from naughty, fattening treats.

Keep me from the cake shop, Lord,
Away from buns and crumpets:
And if a cake is in my hand
give me strength to dump it.

Help me enjoy my salad, Lord,
My yogurt and Ryvita:
Help me to keep in mind one
day my figure will be neater.

# Anyway

People are unreasonable,
illogical and self-centred,
Love them anyway.

If you do good,
people will accuse you
of selfish, ulterior motives.
Love them anyway.

If you are successful,
you win false friends and true enemies.
Succeed anyway.

The good you do today
will be forgotten tomorrow.
Do good anyway.

Honesty and frankness
make you vulnerable.
Be honest and frank anyway.

What you spend years building
may be destroyed overnight.
Build anyway.

People really need help,

but may attack you if you help them.
Help people anyway.

Give the world the best you have and you
will get kicked in the teeth.
Give the world the best you've got anyway.

# When I Am Gone

When I am gone release me, let me go.
I have so many things to do.
Be happy that we had so many years.
I gave you my love, you can only guess
How much you gave me in happiness.
I thank you for the love you have shown,
But now it's time I travelled alone.
So grieve awhile that we must part,
And bless the memories in your heart.
I won't be far away, for life goes on.
And if you need me, call and I will come.
Though you can't see or touch me, I'll be near,
And if you listen with your heart you'll hear
All my love around you, soft and clear.
And then, when you must come this way alone,
I'll greet you with a 'Welcome home'.

# Don't Blame Me –
# Signed: God

...................................

If you destroy this beautiful planet I made for you and the earth is scourged by your horrible weapons of war ...

Don't blame me.

If you keep finding someone to hate, and a way to express that hate causes you to live in anxiety and tension ...

Don't blame me.

If you accumulate things upon things and then live in fear that you may lose them ...

Don't blame me.

If, by your unconcern and lack of compassion for the poor, your taxes are raised to help them ...

Don't blame me.

If you don't take some deliberate time to learn about 'me and you' and 'you and me' and consequently find your life confusing and doubt-filled ...

Don't blame me.

If you don't teach children by good example that 'gifting' their lives for others is the most noble thing they can do, and you end up with grasping politicians and exploiters ...

Don't blame me.

# A Reflection on Living Well

Don't undermine your worth by comparing yourself with others. It is because we are different that each one of us is special.

Don't set your goals by what other people deem important. Only you know what is best for you.

Don't take for granted the things closest to your heart. Cling to them as you would your life, for without them life is meaningless.

Don't let your life slip through your fingers by living in the past. By living your life one day at a time, you live all the days of your life.

Don't give up when you still have something to give. Nothing is really over until the moment you stop trying.

Don't be afraid to admit that you are less than perfect. It is this fragile thread that binds us to each other.

Don't be afraid to encounter risks. It is by taking chances that we learn how to be brave.

Don't shut love out of your life by saying it is impossible to find. The quickest way to receive love is to give love; the fastest way to lose love is to hold it too tightly; and the best way to keep love is to give it wings.

Don't run through life so fast that you forget not only where you've been but also where you're going.

Life is not a race, but a journey to be savoured each step of the way.

# Prayer for Discernment

Grant me, O Lord,
to know what is worth knowing,
To love what is worth loving,
To praise what delights you most,
To value what is precious in your sight,
To hate what is offensive to you.
Do not let me judge by what I see,
Nor pass sentence according to what I hear,
But judge rightly
between things that differ,
And above all to search out
and do what pleases you,
Through Jesus Christ, our Lord.

# God's Love in Creation

Francis of Assisi saw God's love in creation. He talked about Brother Sun and Sister Moon. What he thought centuries ago has become fashionable today. He said everyone has a dignity because everyone is a child of God.

# Why I Love You

...........................................

You come quietly into my private world and let me be.

You really try to understand me when I do not make much sense.

You don't take my problem from me, but trust me to deal with it in my own way.

You give me enough room to discover for myself why I feel upset, and enough time to think for myself what is best.

You allow me the dignity of making my own decisions even though you feel I am wrong.

You don't tell me that funny story you are just bursting to tell me.

You allow me to make my experience one that really matters.

You accept my gratitude by telling me that it is good to know I have been helped.

You grasp my point of view even when it goes against your sincere convictions.

You accept me as I am – warts and all.

You don't offer me religious solace when you sense I am not ready for it.

You look at me, feel for me and really want to know me.

You spend a short, valuable time with me and make me feel it is for ever.

You hold back your desire to give me good advice.

# St Patrick's Breastplate

St Patrick was insistent that there should be one Lord, one faith, one baptism. And that nothing was impossible to God – a God he himself prayed to a hundred times a day.

> May the strength of God guide me this day.
> May his power preserve me.
> May the wisdom of God instruct me.
> And the ear of God hear me.
> The hand of God defend me.
> And may Christ protect me against an
> untimely death.

# St Vincent de Paul on God's Mercy

Always turn your eyes from the study of your own sin to the contemplation of God's mercy. Devote much more thought to the grandeur of his love for you than to your unworthiness towards him, to his strength than to your weakness. When you have done this, surrender yourself into God's arms in the hope that he will make you what he requires you to be and that he will bless all you do.

# This is Me

I accept myself completely.
I accept my strengths and my weaknesses,
My gifts and my shortcomings,
My good points and my faults.
I accept myself completely as a human being.
I accept that I am here to learn and grow,
and I accept that I am learning and
    growing.
I accept the personality I've developed,
and I accept my power to heal and change.
I accept myself without condition or
    reservation.
From this place of strength,
I accept my life fully and I open to the
    lessons it offers me today.
I accept that within my mind are both fear
    and love,
and I accept my power to choose which I
    will experience as real.
I recognise that I experience only the
    results of my own choices.
I accept the times that I choose fear
as part of my learning and healing process,
and I accept that I have the potential and
    power in any moment to choose love
    instead.

I accept mistakes as a part of growth,
so I am always willing to forgive myself
and give myself another chance.
I accept my own life as a blessing and a
gift.
My heart is open to receive, and I am
deeply grateful.
May I always share the gifts that I receive
fully, freely and with joy.

⬥⬥⬥⬥⬥⬥⬥⬥⬥⬥⬥⬥⬥⬥⬥⬥⬥⬥⬥⬥⬥⬥⬥⬥⬥⬥⬥⬥⬥⬥⬥⬥⬥⬥⬥⬥⬥⬥⬥⬥⬥⬥⬥⬥⬥⬥⬥⬥

# You Are Beautiful

Treat yourself the way you are,
and you will remain so.
Treat yourself the way you can become,
and you will become so.
Think freely. Smile often.
Tell those you love that you do.
Hope, grow, give, give in.
Pick some daisies. Keep a promise.
Laugh heartily. Enjoy. Trust life.
Reach out. Let someone in.
Make some mistakes. Learn from them.
Explore the unknown. Believe in yourself.
Celebrate your life! You are beautiful.

# Beatitudes of an Old Person

Happy are they who look at me with kindness.
Happy are they who understand my weary step.
Happy are they who speak loudly
to minimise my deafness.
Happy are they who clasp with warmth
my shaking hands.
Happy are they who take an interest
in my faraway youth.
Happy are they who don't get tired of listening to my
stories, already too many times repeated.
Happy are they who understand my need for affection.
Happy are they who give me fragments of their time.
Happy are they who remember my loneliness.
Happy are they who draw near to me in my suffering.
Happy are they who give me happiness
in this last stage of my life.
Happy are they who are near to me
in the moment of my meeting with the Lord.
When I enter the life without end,
I will remember them in front of the Lord Jesus.

# I'm Special

I'm special.
In all the world there is nobody like me.
Since the beginning of time,
there has never been
another person like me.

Nobody has my smile. Nobody has my eyes,
my nose, my hands, my voice.
I'm special.
I am the only one in all of Creation
who has my set of abilities ...

Through all of eternity no one will ever look,
talk, walk or think like me.
I'm special, I'm rare.
And in all rarity there is a great rare value.

Because of my great rare value,
I need not attempt to imitate others.
I will accept – yes, celebrate – my differences.
Yes, I'm special.

I am beginning to see
that God made me special
for a very special purpose.

God must have a job for me
that no one else can do as I.
Out of all the billions of applicants,
only one is qualified,
only one has the right combination
of what it takes.
That one is me.
Because I'm special.

<br>

◇◇◇◇◇◇◇◇◇◇◇◇◇◇◇◇◇◇◇◇◇◇◇◇◇◇◇◇◇◇◇◇◇◇◇◇◇◇◇◇◇◇◇◇◇

# Holiness

Holiness does not come from doing good. Rather we do good because we are holy.

Holiness is not the avoidance of evil. Rather we avoid evil because we are holy.

Holiness is not the result of constant prayer. We pray because we are holy.

Holiness is not a gift we obtain after a lifetime of service. Rather we give service because we are holy.

Jesus said it all in Matthew's gospel when he said: 'I was hungry and you gave me food. I was thirsty and you gave me drink. I was a stranger and you welcomed me. I was naked and you gave me clothing. I was sick and you took care of me. I was in prison and you visited me ... As long as you did it to one of my brethren, then you did it to me.'

# From Mother to Child

........................

I gave you life,
but cannot live it for you.
I can give you directions,
but I cannot force you to follow them.

I can take you to church each Sunday,
but I cannot make you believe.
I can give you love,
but I cannot make you take it.

I can teach you to share,
but I cannot make you unselfish.
I can teach you respect,
but I cannot force you to be honourable.

I can advise you about friends,
but cannot choose them for you.
I can advise you about sex,
but I cannot keep you pure.

I can tell you about alcohol and drugs,
but I cannot say 'no' for you.
I can teach you about kindness,
but I cannot force you to be courteous.

I can pray for you,
but I cannot make you walk with God.
I can tell you how to live,
but I cannot give you eternal life.
I can love you with unconditional love all
    of my life
and I always will.

# Change Yourself First

The following words were found inscribed on the tomb of an Anglican bishop who was buried in Westminster Abbey.

'When I was young and free and my imagination had no limits, I dreamed of changing the world.

As I grew older and wiser I discovered the world would not change. So I shortened my sights somewhat and decided to change only my country. But it too seemed immovable.

As I grew into my twilight years in one last desperate attempt, I settled for changing my family, those closest to me, but alas they would have none of it.

And now, as I lie on my deathbed, I suddenly realise: if I had only changed myself first, then by example I would have changed my family.

And from their inspiration and encouragement I would have been able to better my country and, who knows, I may even have bettered the world.'

# How Often?

How often do we think that God's not
    listening to our prayers?
How often do we feel neglected, feel that
    no one cares?
How often do we beg, beseech, for answers
    to our call? How often do we do we
    think that there's no one there at all?
Do we never stop and thank the Lord for
    each new dawning day?
Do we never stop and thank him for the
    friends he sends our way?
Do we never stop and thank him for his
    beauty all around?
Do we never stop and realise, his loving
    knows no bounds?
Our every prayer is answered in the
    whispers of the wind.
Our every prayer is answered in
    forgiveness of our sins.
Our every prayer is answered in the
    blessings we can't see.
Our every prayer should simply be:
    'Thy will be done to me.'

# Prayer of a Native American

........................

May I Walk in Beauty and Wisdom, O
    Great Spirit,
Whose voice I hear in the winds
And whose breath gives life to the world.
Hear me.
I come to you as one of your many children.
I am small and weak,
I need your strength and your wisdom.
May I walk in beauty.
May my eyes ever behold the red and
    purple sunset.
May my hands respect the things you have
    made.
Make my ears sharp to hear your voice.
Make me wise so that I may know
The things you have taught your children,
The lessons you have hidden in every leaf
    and rock.
Make me strong,
So that I may not be superior to other
    people,
But able to fight my greatest enemy,
Which is myself.
Make me ever ready to come to you with
    straight eyes,

So that when life fades as the fading
    sunset,
My spirit may come to you without shame.

---

# An Honest Prayer

Dear God, So far today I've done OK.
I haven't gossiped, or lost my temper.
I haven't been grumpy, nasty or selfish.
But – in a few more minutes, God,
I'm going to get out of bed,
And that's when I will need your help!
Amen